VICE PRESIDENTS, PRESIDENTIAL ELECTIONS, AND THE MEDIA

VICE PRESIDENTS, PRESIDENTIAL ELECTIONS, AND THE MEDIA

Second Fiddles in the Spotlight

Stacy G. Ulbig

FIRST**FORUM**PRESS

A DIVISION OF LYNNE RIENNER PUBLISHERS, INC. • BOULDER & LONDON

Published in the United States of America in 2013 by
FirstForumPress
A division of Lynne Rienner Publishers, Inc.
1800 30th Street, Boulder, Colorado 80301
www.firstforumpress.com

and in the United Kingdom by
FirstForumPress
A division of Lynne Rienner Publishers, Inc.
3 Henrietta Street, Covent Garden, London WC2E 8LU

Library of Congress Cataloging-in-Publication Data
Ulbig, Stacy G.
  Vice presidents, presidential elections, and the media: second fiddles in
the spotlight/Stacy G. Ulbig.
  Includes bibliographical references and index.
  ISBN 978-1-935049-56-2 (alk. paper)
  1. Vice-Presidents—United States. 2. Vice-Presidential
candidates—United States. 3. Vice-Presidents—United States—Election.
4. United States—Politics and government. I. Title.
  JK609.5.U43 2013
  324.973—dc23
2012047131

British Cataloguing in Publication Data
A Cataloguing in Publication record for this book
is available from the British Library.

This book was produced from digital files prepared by the author
using the FirstForumComposer.

Printed and bound in the United States of America

 The paper used in this publication meets the requirements
of the American National Standard for Permanence of
Paper for Printed Library Materials Z39.48-1992.

5 4 3 2 1

Contents

Tables and Figures

Figures

Acknowledgments

Though only my name appears as author of this book, many others deserve credit for its existence as well. While I am certain to forget at least one or two of the many people who helped and supported me throughout the writing of the book, I would like to thank a number of people for their contributions. To those I have forgotten, please forgive me.

This project began as an article that was published in the journal *American Politics Research* in 2010. Thanks go to the anonymous reviewers of the manuscript of the article, who provided much needed critical advice about the earliest stages of this research, and to then editor Jim Gimpel for giving me the opportunity to revise a rather rough first submission into something worthy of seeing the light of day.

That article would never have become anything more without the encouragement of Jessica Gribble, acquisitions editor at Lynne Rienner Publishers. After making the audacious suggestion that I could produce a book-length manuscript, she gave me the necessary support to actually complete the task. Somehow Jessica was able to give me the space to work, without ever being more than an email or phone call away when I needed guidance and advice. Among the many things that she did was find amazing reviewers for my manuscript. The questions, advice, and suggestions those reviewers provided resulted in some of the best parts of the book.

Special thanks also go to the Office of Sponsored Research at Sam Houston State University for supporting this project with a summer Faculty Research Grant. Without that grant, data collection for the project would have been unlikely, if not impossible. The grant afforded me the opportunity to employ the talents of several graduate students: I cannot thank Charles Smith and Ashley Moulder enough for the considerable time they spent reading and coding newspaper articles for this project. Nor can I ever fully convey my appreciation for the many times Mike Smith read drafts of the manuscript. In those dark hours when I least wanted to work on the project, the enthusiasm of these students rallied my spirits and got me back on task.

A number of individuals who stood beside me throughout the lengthy process of writing the book also deserve some recognition. This project would probably not exist at all if not for Johanna Dunaway. The question of whether, or when, vice presidential candidates matter to voters arose during a road trip to Baton Rouge, Louisiana, back in the days leading up to the 2008 presidential election. Johanna's constant support and advice were invaluable. Every student at LSU should make a point of taking a class from Dr. Dunaway.

From the time the project was nothing more than an idea for a conference paper, Justin Fuller served as a sounding board and critic. Our many lunchtime conversations birthed some of the more creative aspects of this work, and Justin's careful reading and re-reading of various drafts of the manuscript improved its quality dramatically. He has taught me a lot over the years.

I have also had the good fortune to have some incredible people as colleagues. Joel Paddock served as an unwavering supporter during my time at Missouri State University, and his assurance that I was up to the task of writing a book gave me the confidence to take on the project. Heather Evans and Lauren Edwards offered much needed advice along the way, and they were always able to act excited about the project when I cornered them and made them talk with me about it. Thanks, ladies.

Mitzi Mahoney was along on that road trip when the idea for this project developed. In the following years, she was a constant source of support and encouragement. Mitzi has the ability to make me laugh when I feel least able to, and she somehow knew how to inquire about progress on the project at just the right intervals.

Rhonda Callaway has influenced this project more than she knows. Her ready advice and counseling at every turn were invaluable. More important, however, she provided an example of how a person can persevere through the roughest of times without ever losing faith. Thanks also have to go out to her parents for raising her to be this way.

Finally, thanks go to my personal support staff. When I told Bob Barnhill that I could see the finish line and this book might actually be published, he replied, "I never thought there was a doubt." He believes in me when I don't believe in myself, and he put up with me through this project even after having endured the dissertation writing years. Before there was Bob, there were my parents, Becky and Boyce Ulbig. I cannot thank them enough for raising me to believe that I can do what I put my mind to and giving me the skills to actually get it done. Then there is Jitterbug, who taught me, among other things, that no matter how long and difficult the trail looks you should wag your tail and start walking. You never know what wonderful things you'll discover along the way.

1

Do Voters Care About Vice Presidents?

At a campaign rally on his 72nd birthday, Presidential candidate John McCain introduced American voters to the woman some have called a "moose-hunting hockey mom and former mayor of Wasilla, Alaska," (Katz 2008) as his running mate in the 2008 presidential election. American voters responded with a collective, "who?" and then proceeded to bombard their internet search engines with the name "Sarah Palin" (PR Newswire 2008). Five days later, more than 37 million people sat in front of their televisions where they met the woman they had been speculating about as she delivered an acceptance speech "full of moxie" at the Republican National Convention (McCarthy 2008). The public remained intensely interested in Palin when she followed up her strong Convention performance with lackluster—some would say embarrassing—public appearances and became the target of late night talk show hosts and the writers at *Saturday Night Live*.

There is little doubt Sarah Palin received more attention than vice presidential candidates normally do. Debate rages, however, about just how much she actually mattered in the 2008 Presidential campaign. While some saw McCain's selection of Palin as "[t]he most fateful decision [he] ever made" (The Richmonder 2008) and claimed she was "probably the most damaging vice-Presidential nominee in American history" (Chait 2010), others pointed out how unfair it is to isolate Palin for the ticket's loss given McCain's many challenges in the election (Daniels 2008).

Rating McCain's choice of Sarah Palin as a vice presidential running mate as the second of the top ten reasons why McCain lost the 2008 Presidential election, Richmond (2008) points to Palin's failure to assure voters she was capable of serving as vice president, and perhaps eventually president, as the reason many voters turned away from the ticket. Similarly, Chusid (2008) points out the ways in which Palin alienated Independent voters, ultimately pushing them toward the Obama-Biden ticket. Taking on the question of why economic conditions failed to explain the outcome of the 2008 election as they had in most previous presidential contests, Johnston and Thorson (2009) argue "the answer to this question starts with Sarah Palin." Noting that "vote intentions were closely tied to Palin's approval ratings" through most of the campaign, they view Palin's influence on voters as the factor that most precisely predicted McCain's electoral support. Given these perspectives, it is perhaps no surprise Richmond (2008) concluded that "Sarah Palin . . . was probably the biggest mistake John McCain made."

Countering the avalanche of blame targeted at Palin, political scientist James Campbell reminded the public that the bottom of the ticket rarely means much to voters. "We know that [vice presidential candidates] don't matter and that they don't have a direct effect on the vote," he said in an interview early in the 2008 campaign season (Liasson 2008). Recalling Lyndon Johnson's ability to bring Texas's valuable electoral votes to the Kennedy ticket, he pointed out that it had been nearly 50 years since a vice presidential nominee actually made a difference in an election. He also reminded listeners of Dan Quayle's poor rapport with the public as evidence that even when the public takes a negative view of a vice presidential candidate, the ticket still often wins. Empirical research largely supports Campbell's assertions, with Brox and Cassells (2009) noting how unlikely it was that "Palin had much of an impact on presidential voting" (360) since she failed to influence the votes of women or to help distance her ticket from the legacy of the Bush administration. Even when researchers isolate the ways in which Palin probably did cost McCain votes, they typically conclude that "Palin's campaign performance did not necessarily change the election outcome" (Elis, Hillygus, and Nie 2010: 589). Estimates suggest that negative voter feelings about Palin cost McCain about 1.6 percentage points on Election Day, but since Obama's winning margin was seven percentage points, it seems unlikely Palin, alone, caused the Republican loss. So, it is not surprising that some, like New Jersey Governor Chris Christie, believe that "in the end nobody votes for vice president, they vote for president" (ABC News 2012).

The countervailing views expressed about Palin's influence in the 2008 Presidential election highlight a conundrum of modern American presidential politics. Even though many believe vice presidential candidates hold only minor import for most voters, the vice presidential candidates are often treated as if they can play such a meaningful role in voter decision making as to change an election outcome. These conflicting views remain pervasive because each contains some element of truth. Most of the time vice presidential candidates are nothing more than second fiddles, playing little role in the ultimate decisions voters make; however, there are instances when some vice presidential candidates take center stage and play a very large part in helping voters decide how to cast their ballots. So who cares about these second fiddles and why?

The research presented in this book highlights the variable impact vice presidential candidates of the past 40 years have had on voters and examines the role that the media plays in making some of them more electorally important than others. Throughout, I draw on established research about the important role of information in campaigns, the media's role in conveying this information and priming voters to consider some elements of the campaign more than others, and the ways in which individual-level partisanship can mute these media effects.

What Part Do Second Fiddles Play?

Every four years journalists and academics alike engage in a riveting game of "veepstakes," attempting to guess the eventual vice presidential nominees on each ticket. While much wild speculation flies about exactly who the eventual nominee will be, the general consensus is that electoral imperatives compel the selection of vice presidential candidates. The actual qualifications of the candidate to serve as president if called upon have traditionally been viewed as inconsequential. The selection of a vice presidential candidate, it is argued, "is far more likely to be based on short-term electoral calculations than on long-term governance considerations" (Sigelman and Wahlbeck 2008: 855). Such was the case in 1988 when George H.W. Bush considered dropping Dan Quayle for actor Clint Eastwood as his running mate for the presidency (Dwyer 2011). Lagging opponent Michael Dukakis by more than 15 points in the polls, Bush seriously, though briefly, considered opting for Eastwood, a Republican mayor, in an effort to stir some voter excitement about the ticket. In fact, the idea that that the person occupying the bottom of the ticket serves as nothing more than an electoral marketing device used to secure votes (Witcover 1992; Sigelman and Wahlbeck 2008) has been so strong that some believe that "[i]f elected, the vice president could look forward to being replaced four years later" when a different vice presidential candidate might prove more electorally beneficial (Nelson 1988: 859).

When it comes to getting elected, presenting voters with a balanced ticket seems to be the driving force behind vice presidential candidate selection (e.g., Goldstein 1982; Natoli 1985; Nelson 1988a and b; Polsby and Wildavsky 2012; Pomper 1963). "[T]he conventional wisdom is that presidential candidates seek to balance their ticket by choosing a running mate who contributes key qualities that the presidential nominee lacks" (Hiller and Kriner 2008: 402). For instance, an older presidential candidate will choose a younger running mate, a less politically experienced presidential candidate will choose someone with a long and credible political career to join the ticket, or a liberal presidential candidate will seek a moderate, or even conservative, partner. Studies have validated that vice presidential candidates who strike a balance with the presidential candidate on factors such as age, experience, ideology, gender, race, religion, or state or regional affiliation stand a better chance of being asked to join the ticket (Baumgartner 2008; Bryce 1893; Goldstein 1982; Hiller and Kriner 2008; Hurwitz 1980; Mayer 2000; Sigelman and Wahlbeck 1997; Watson and Yon 2006).

While there are any number of potential factors on which a ticket might be balanced, geographical region and home state represent the factors most frequently emphasized by scholars (Dudley and Rapoport 1989; Goldstein 1982; Hiller and Kriner 2008; Witcover 1977). Selecting a running mate from a different region of the country than the presidential candidate, it is argued, can "[shore] up support for the nomination among party factions and [mollify] any lingering intrapartisan divisions after the convention as the critical fall campaign season approache[s]" (Hiller and Kriner 2008: 404; see also Rohde 1991). Offering the bottom of the ticket to a candidate from a populous state holds the promise of securing a good number of precious electoral votes (Adkison 1992). As Sigelman and Wahlbeck (1997) point out, "the temptation to 'go hunting where the ducks are' is virtually irresistible for an electorally motivated politician" (857). The 1960 Kennedy-Johnson ticket epitomizes both of these concerns (Hiller and Kriner 2008). Hailing from a Southern state, Johnson offered the opportunity to reach across a long-standing intra-party faction and stem third party challenges from conservative Southern Democrats who were displeased with Kennedy's nomination. As a bonus, Johnson's populous home state of Texas offered the possible reward of a large number of valuable electoral votes.

Contrasting the considerable efforts put into forecasting the selection of vice presidential candidates, there is relatively little empirical work on the importance of these candidates once they are named. The scant existing research into the actual impact that vice presidential candidates have on aggregate electoral outcomes offers mixed findings. While some studies have failed to identify any vice presidential home state advantage, others isolate some minimal effects. Neither Holbrook (1991) nor Dudley and Rappaport (1989) locate any substantial evidence of "the 'friends and neighbors' effects in vice presidential candidates' home state" (Dudley and Rappaport 1989: 540), though the latter did find some effects in small states. And while Campbell (1992) found vice presidential home state to be related to electoral success, this factor was among the weakest of the sixteen predictor variables he studied. Similarly, others have discovered only a small (2-2.5%) "home state bump" in votes that can be attributed to vice presidential candidates (Campbell, Ali, and Jalazai 2006; Garand 1988; Holbrook 1991; Lewis-Beck and Rice 1983; Rosenstone 1983).

Vice presidential impact on individual-level vote choice has been just as elusive to capture. There is some evidence that voters' perceptions of vice presidential candidates do indeed have an impact on vote choice, though it is likely a small one. Adkison (1982) finds that feelings about the bottom of the ticket can affect vote choice, but that the "running mate usually hurts a ticket but does not help it much" (333). Although Frankovic (1984) found that voters who took vice presidential candidates into consideration favored the Mondale-Ferraro ticket, the extremely small impact this had led her to conclude that the vice presidential candidates "mattered only marginally in the public's final voting decision" (47). Similarly, Wattenberg (1984; 1995) finds a connection between voters' evaluations of vice presidential candidates and their ultimate vote choices but concludes that the effect is likely a small one affecting only about 0.75 percent of the presidential vote share or less. At the same time, others (Romero 2004) can isolate no connection between voter perceptions of vice presidential candidates and ultimate vote choice. Results such as these have led some to argue that "[t]here is little evidence to suggest that vice presidents add greatly to or detract severely from the popularity of presidential candidates with voters" (Polsby and Wildavsky 2012: 142).

On the whole, scholars tend to simultaneously argue that politicians give great consideration to the electoral significance that vice presidential candidates might play but concede that those at the bottom of the ticket remain little more than afterthoughts in voters' minds on Election Day. These electoral second fiddles, it seems, must prove worthy to join the orchestra but end up playing only minor parts in the symphony of presidential election campaigns.

When Might Second Fiddles Matter?

Why is it that most vice presidential candidates matter so little to voters while a few of those occupying the bottom of the ticket come to command so much voter attention? In this book, I attempt to explain why vice presidential candidates typically do not have an impact on voters, and yet, why sometimes they do. Relying on an informational theory of elections, I argue that the variable impact of vice presidential candidates can be explained, at least in part, by the varying amounts of information voters have about them. Voters are likely to consider candidates they know better than those they have heard little about. Since voters receive most of their campaign information from the mass media, I focus on the media attention given to these candidates as the key explanatory factor. I argue that heightened media attention to vice presidential candidates during the Presidential campaign primes voters to consider their feelings about these candidates more when making a vote choice. Vice presidential candidates covered more heavily by the media will mean more to voters and thus have a larger impact on their ultimate vote choice.

In the chapters that follow, I investigate the varying impact vice presidential candidates have had on voters in presidential elections over the past four decades. Examining all presidential elections from 1972 to 2008, I illustrate the important role media coverage plays in giving some vice presidential candidates more electoral impact than others. Along the way, I highlight important distinctions with regard to the types of media coverage likely to be most important, as well as the types of voters most likely to be affected by such coverage.

In the next chapter, I take on three main questions. Given the general impression that vice presidential candidates have little electoral impact, I first answer the question of why we should expect vice presidential candidates to affect voter decision making at all. After reviewing arguments about why those at the bottom of the ticket should or should not affect voter decision making, I develop a theory of how media coverage will make some vice presidential candidates more meaningful to voters than others. Second, I approach the question of which voters should be most affected by vice presidential candidates. Given the importance of the media in exposing voters to vice presidential candidates, I explore the differential impact that media portrayals of vice presidential candidates have on partisans and non-partisans. I argue that media messages will most strongly affect voters lacking pre-existing partisan allegiances, and thus these voters will be most likely to react to media portrayals of vice presidential candidates.

Finally, I explore the empirical question of how much vice presidential candidates have actually affected the vote choice of partisan and nonpartisan voters over time. After establishing a measure of vice presidential impact, I review the varied impact of vice presidential candidates from 1972 to 2008.

This measure of vice presidential impact serves as the dependent variable in the analyses that follow, with chapters 3-5 presenting investigations into the causes of the varied impact that vice presidential candidates have had. In chapter 3, I start to unravel the mystery about why some vice presidential candidates matter more to voters than others by asking whether candidates receiving more media coverage have a greater impact on voters than those receiving less media attention. After reviewing the arguments about the importance of campaign information in voter decision making, I draw on media priming research to explain how increased media attention to vice presidential candidates can cause voters to more readily consider their feelings about these candidates when making a vote choice. I then measure the amount of media coverage given to the bottom of the ticket over time, illustrating that some vice presidential candidates have received more media attention than others. Using this measure, I find that vice presidential candidates who draw more (and more intense) media coverage exert a stronger impact on voter decision making.

In chapter 4, I move beyond the sheer amount of media coverage to investigate whether the tone of media portrayals matters. After discussing the research that suggests voters tend to weigh negative information about candidates more heavily than positive information, I develop measures of media negativity and test to see if such coverage leads voters to consider some vice presidential candidates more than others. Somewhat surprisingly, I find that negative coverage of candidates in presidential elections plays little role in accounting for why some vice presidential candidates have mattered more to voters than others. Importantly, however, negative media coverage plays quite a large role in explaining the electoral impact of incumbent vice presidential candidates at reelection time.

In chapter 5, I explore whether media attention to candidates' sociodemographic characteristics seems to account for the impact these candidates have on voters. After reviewing the literature about how voters use such characteristics as information shortcuts, I examine the connection between media coverage of candidates' race, sex, religious preference, and marital status and vice presidential impact on voters. The findings show that when the media focuses more on a vice presidential candidate's sex or religious preference (and to a lesser degree, his/her marital status), especially in a negative way, voters are more likely to let the candidate affect their vote choice.

Finally, in chapter 6 I ask whether media coverage of vice presidential candidates' personality traits seem to explain why some of these candidates matter more than others to voters. I first review the ways in which job-related personality traits have been shown to influence voting in presidential elections, and then I investigate the connection of media coverage of candidate traits traditionally important to voters and the impact of vice presidential candidates. Findings reveal that while the overall amount of attention the media gives to candidate traits does not increase candidate impact on voters, more negative coverage of two key vice presidential traits (political experience and intelligence) leads voters to consider some candidates more than others when casting a ballot.

I bring all this research together in the concluding chapter where I review key findings and non-findings from the previous chapters, tying them to the existing academic knowledge about presidential elections, the role of the media, and the importance of religion and gender in American politics. I then discuss the historical importance of vice presidential candidates in elections of the past four decades, highlighting the reasons why four vice presidential candidates came to exert a much stronger impact on voters than others. I conclude by speculating about how the findings presented in this book speak to the role vice presidential candidates are likely to play in future elections.

2

The Varying Impact of Vice Presidential Candidates

While accepted wisdom says vice presidential candidates matter little to voters, it is also the case that some VP candidates come to play a very meaningful role in voter decision making. Why is it that some second fiddles play louder than others? In this chapter, I seek to explain three things: (1) why we might expect most vice presidential candidates to play little, if any, role in voter decision making, (2) when we might expect those at the bottom of the ticket to become more important to voters, and (3) which voters we might expect to be most attentive to these candidates. With these questions addressed, I then develop and explore a measure of the impact that vice presidential candidates have had on voters since the 1970s.

Should Vice Presidential Candidates Matter?

There are good reasons to believe that vice presidential candidates should not play much of a role in shaping voter decision making. These candidates typically receive far less media coverage than their presidential running mates. Patterns of press coverage since 1972 indicate that presidential candidates receive about three and a half times as much coverage as vice presidential candidates.[1] Consequently, voters probably have very little information about the bottom of the ticket to consider when making a vote choice. Even when VP candidates take center stage in their own debates, there is little evidence that they "do much at all to alter the political landscape" (Holbrook 1996: 109). The small impact that the vice presidential debates seem to have disappears rather quickly, and it is usually long gone before Election Day. Some have also suggested that even though the office of the vice presidency has taken on more responsibilities, "these responsibilities are still largely ceremonial" and vice presidents still offer "disparaging descriptions" of the office (Romero 2004: 456). If voters are aware of these facts, it argues against considerations about VP candidates weighing very heavily on vote choice.

Common wisdom assumes that vice presidential candidates typically mean little to the eventual election outcome. In fact, some have suggested "a 72-hour rule of thumb for running mates: if they are still on the front page three days after their nomination, it means there's a problem" (Turque, et al. 2000: 29). Poll results suggest much the same, with voters typically indicating that the VP candidate is of little importance to them when they vote. Typically about eight to fifteen percent of voters polled indicate that the vice presidential candidate was an important consideration for them when they cast their ballot (Frankovic 1984; Wattenberg 1995). Even in the 2008 election, when media discussion of the VP candidates was running high, two-thirds of voters contended that John McCain and Barack Obama's running mates would mean little to them when it came to making their vote choice (CBS News Poll 2008). Even the multitude of election forecasting models that accompany presidential elections typically ignore the potential impact of vice presidential candidates, focusing instead on factors such as presidential popularity, economic perceptions, whether the nation is at war, and candidate incumbency (see, for instance, the Symposia that have appeared for the last three elections in *PS: Political Science and Politics*).[2]

Still, there are some reasons to believe that veeps, at least sometimes, do play a role in influencing vote choice. There are at least two moments in the campaign when the media focuses much attention on those occupying the bottom of the ticket – at convention time when the nominees are announced and when vice presidential candidates participate in televised debates (Romero 2004). Voters could absorb information during these times that, if striking enough, could remain with them in the voting booth. In fact, there is evidence that when media coverage of Biden and Palin increased around the VP debate, voters' ratings of the candidates responded (Kenski 2010). And, more telling, "Palin's favorability ratings had the strongest association with vote preference during the 13-day period following the third presidential debate and during the last 3 days of the campaign" (Kenski 2010: 235). Further, the media have increasingly covered the ticket as a team. Consequently, "[i]t is reasonable to hypothesize that, because voters are exposed to a two-person team, the popularity of each player should have an impact on their vote decisions" (Wattenberg 1995: 505).

Further, voters might recognize the increased responsibilities and prestige of the vice presidency, however superficial they may be, and bring considerations about the candidates likely to occupy that office to bear on their vote choice. Though once considered "the most insignificant office that ever the invention of man contrived or his imagination conceived" (John Adams, as quoted in Rossiter 1948: 384), the modern vice presidency has gained tremendous power (see e.g., Goldstein 1982; Light 1984; Mayer 2000; Nelson 1988a). Beginning with the passage of the National Security Act of 1947, vice presidents have assumed increasing governmental responsibilities (Pomper 1966; Williams 1956). Modern vice presidents "can be expected to serve routinely as deputy chiefs of state . . . to be available for service at any time as deputy to the President in the field of foreign affairs" (David 1967: 721). Since at least the Carter administration vice presidents have been included as important members of the governing team (Light 1984), and "Vice President Richard Cheney's unprecedented power in the administration of George W. Bush . . . is only the latest manifestation of the newly invigorated office" (Hiller and Kriner 2008: 401). Given the heightened powers of the office, voters are likely to consider the competency of those at the bottom of the ticket more seriously than ever before.

Similarly, many argue that voters seriously anticipate the current vice presidential candidate eventually becoming president, at least since former vice president Richard Nixon's bid for the presidency in 1960 (Pomper 1966; Romero 2004). Though the vice presidency was once viewed as a "political dead end" (Hurwitz 1980: 509) or "a hollow shell of an office, an impotent and uncomfortable heir apparent sought by practically no one we should like to see as President," (Rossiter 1948: 383), the office has more recently become a viable stepping stone to presidential nomination. Even if the incumbent vice president exhibits potential weaknesses, he "automatically becomes a serious possibility for the next presidential nomination" (Matthews 1974: 44; see also, Graham 1974). And with eight vice presidents succeeding presidents who died in office, history has illustrated the importance of having a vice president who "would be a great president if [the president] dropped dead, got shot, was in a plane crash" (Bill Clinton, as quoted in Hiller and Kriner 2008: 407). When it comes to electoral strategies, those running presidential campaigns certainly agree that a presidential candidate's age can "heighten his need to choose somebody whom voters would feel comfortable with as president should anything happen to him" (Cooper 2008). Both Ronald Reagan and John McCain, the two oldest candidates to seek the presidency, consciously chose VP candidates who would allay voter concern about the possibility of a ninth vice presidential succession. As one veteran campaign staffer argued, concern about Reagan's age "wouldn't go away until the day he picked George Bush as vice president. And then people said, well, here's a known quantity, the guy has experience, including international experience, and yeah, he could handle it" (Cooper 2008). And many believe that questions about Palin's ability to assume the presidency cost McCain key voter support in the election (Elis, Hillygus, and Nie 2010; Kenski 2010). Thus, many argue that "the best politics is to select a person who is actually perceived by the American people as being qualified and able to serve as president if that became necessary" (Witcover 1977: 361; see also Nelson 1988b).

Theoretically, then, it seems that feelings about vice presidential candidates are likely to influence vote choice more at some times than others. When voters become aware of VP candidates, they are more likely to form impressions of them, and these feelings are likely to subsequently impact vote choice. History suggests, however, that voters do not always take notice of the bottom of the ticket.

Information, the Media, and Vice Presidential Candidates

Throughout the remainder of this book, I argue that the level and type of media coverage garnered by vice presidential candidates explains why some have meant more to voters than others. In doing so, I rely on Zaller's (1989) theoretical concept of "differential information flow" in campaigns. Campaigns, he explained "consist of multiple messages that may penetrate differentially far into the mass electorate" (Zaller 1989: 181). Voters are bombarded with "bundles of competing messages" (Zaller 1989: 182), some of which reach them more strongly than others. The messages that reach voters are likely to influence their vote decisions while those that fail to "penetrate the electorate" (Zaller 1989: 182) play no role in shaping decision making. I argue that this basic theoretical mechanism helps to explain why some VP candidates matter more to voters than others.

Vice presidential candidates can only matter to voters when they know and care about them. In the "bundle of competing messages" voters receive during presidential campaigns, messages about VP candidates often get drowned out by messages about other campaign elements, such as presidential candidates, salient issues, or scandals. Consequently, in many elections very little information about the bottom of the ticket makes its way to voters. Without information on these candidates, voters fail to take them into consideration in the voting booth. Sometimes, however, messages about VP candidates come through loud and clear. In these situations, voters are likely to rely on the information they have about the candidate and take it into consideration when casting their ballot. This differential information flow helps to explain why some vice presidential candidates matter more to voters than others. When voters have information about VP candidates, they matter. When information about them is scarce, they do not.

Any discussion of information flow during campaigns would not be complete without the inclusion of the mass media. During election season, voters rely on the media to provide them with information about the "policy positions, qualities, and abilities of the candidates," making the media "the primary conduits for information on the campaigns" (Dalton, Beck, Huckfeldt 1998: 111). In conveying such information, the media influences the factors voters take into consideration (Iyengar 1991, Iyengar and Kinder 1987, Patterson 1993). By highlighting some aspects of the campaign more than others, the media leads voters to consider those aspects more heavily when making their vote choices (Kelleher and Wolack 2006). When the media emphasized a particular issue such as the Persian Gulf War (Krosnick and Brannon 1993) or the economy (Hetherington 1996) in the 1992 election, voters considered these issues more heavily when making their vote choices. Similarly, when the media discusses the candidates' integrity, leadership, or empathy more frequently, voters allow their perceptions of these traits to more greatly influence their votes (see e.g., Druckman 2004; Druckman and Holmes 204; Funk 1999; Jacobs and Shapiro 1994; McGraw and Ling 2003; Mendelsohn 1996).

These effects likely translate to vice presidential candidates as well. Just as a media focus on a war, economic conditions, or a candidate's personal traits can lead voters to more seriously consider those factors when casting a ballot, heightened media coverage of a VP candidate can lead voters to weigh their impressions of that candidate more heavily in the voting booth. When the media focuses on a vice presidential candidate more, voters will know more about that candidate and be more likely to consider their feelings about him/her when making a vote decision.

Thus, in elections with little media coverage of the bottom of the ticket, voters are less likely to be aware of candidates and are less likely to form impressions of them. Conversely, in those times when the media readily presents these candidates to the public, voters develop feelings about the potential vice presidents that go on to affect their vote choices. Since not all VP candidates garner media attention to the same degree, feelings about some candidates will be more closely associated with vote choice than others.

The Conditional Nature of Media Effects

Given the centrality of media coverage, it is important to remember that not all members of the electorate are swayed by the media to the same extent. The impact of feelings about vice presidential candidates is likely to be limited primarily to the portion of the electorate most susceptible to media influence. When it comes to presidential elections, non-partisans represent perhaps the most persuadable group. These voters are interested and aware enough to cast a ballot, but "[w]ithout a party attachment to anchor their choice, Independents should be more likely to start the campaign with an open mind about the two candidates" (Hillygus and Shields 2008: 25). Voters claiming allegiance to neither major party are likely to make their vote choice later in the campaign (and thus spend more time exposed to media messages), be more open to media messages concerning all candidates, and be most affected by the messages they are hearing (see e.g., Campbell, et al 1960; Zaller 1992). Thus, these voters' awareness and impressions of VP candidates are likely to be greatly affected by media coverage. Conversely, partisans are likely to make their vote choice very early in the campaign season, be open primarily to media messages favorable to their preferred candidates, and be largely unaffected by other media messages (see e.g., Bartels 2002; Campbell, et al 1960; Taber and Lodge 2006; Zaller 1992). Partisans are much more likely to be aware of the candidates even in the absence of media coverage, and their impressions of the candidates are likely formed well before any media coverage begins. Given the varied impact that media coverage is likely to have, it is reasonable to expect that campaign effects, including feelings about vice presidential candidates and media coverage of these candidates, will be strongest among voters who call themselves Independents.

Measuring the Impact of Vice Presidential Candidates

If we are to understand why some vice presidential candidates mean more to voters than others, we must first find a way to establish how much these candidates actually do affect voter decision making. The traditional approach to capturing the impact that vice presidential candidates have on voters is to simply ask voters if they consider the vice president when considering who to support in the presidential election. Sometimes voters are asked in exit polls to reveal which of a list of factors, often including the VP candidates, "mattered most" when they were making their vote choice (Frankovic 1984). Other times voters are asked to rate the presidential candidate's choice of a running mate (ABC News 2000; Gallup Poll 2000) or if the VP candidate will make them "more likely, less likely, or won't make any difference" in their vote choice (Gallup Poll 2000).

While this approach is certainly a direct one, it has the shortcoming of not fully capturing the more subtle ways in which feelings about vice presidential candidates might be influencing voter choice. As has been illustrated repeatedly, information and attitudes that even the voters themselves are not aware of frequently influence vote choice. For instance, while a large majority of voters say they would vote for a qualified woman as president, when given the chance in experiments voters tend to prefer the equally qualified male candidate (see e.g., Rosenwasser and Seale 1988; Rosenwasser and Dean 1989; Smith, Paul, and Paul 2007; Paul and Smith 2008). Similarly, even though far fewer survey respondents will readily admit racist attitudes than in the past (Schuman, et al 1997), more subtle forms of implicit prejudice abound (Olson and Fazio 2003; Gawronski and Bodenhausen 2006; Nosek, et al 2007). Though many deny that such racist attitudes play a role in their behavior, a number of studies have shown that "individual differences in implicit prejudice predict discriminatory behavior," including vote choice (Payne, et al 2010: 367).

Given the potential shortcoming of using a traditional survey measure of vice presidential candidate impact, I seek to establish candidate impact on vote choice in a more subtle manner. Instead of asking voters if they consider their feelings about the VP candidate when voting, I predict the impact that such feelings actually had on their ultimate vote choice. When the feelings a voter holds about a vice presidential candidate prove to be strongly related to their vote in the presidential election, then VP impact is said to be high. Conversely, when feelings about the VP candidate play little role in predicting vote choice, the candidate impact is considered low.

I rely on the well-established American National Election Studies (ANES) time series dataset to measure the attitudes and behavior of voters. Conducted since 1948, the ANES polls a random sample of American voters about a range of political attitudes and behaviors both before and after each presidential election.[3] Used in countless studies of American elections, the dataset represents "the gold standard for understanding the politics of our democracy" (Institute for Social Research 2010). The data offer high quality measurements of public opinion that are comparable across years.

To establish the impact that attitudes toward vice presidential candidates have on vote choice, I use ANES data for all presidential elections between 1972 and 2008.[4] For each candidate in each election, I perform statistical analyses to predict individual-level vote choice with feelings about the presidential and VP candidates, as well as a number of other relevant voter attitudes and characteristics. I then interpret the statistical results to determine the impact that feelings about the vice presidential candidate had on voters in each election.

To predict the impact that feelings about VP candidates had on vote choice, I perform a series of multivariate regressions predicting vote choice with feelings about presidential and vice presidential candidates. Multivariate regression is a statistical technique that allows us to assess the relationship between two factors while accounting for the possible influence of additional variables. In this case, I investigate the relationship between vote choice and feelings about candidates while controlling for other factors that have been shown to influence voter decision making. If, after accounting for the possible influence of these additional factors, feelings about VP candidates exhibit a relationship with vote choice then we have more assurance that these feelings are indeed causing, at least in part, the decisions that voters make.

Individual vote choice represents the dependent variable in this analysis – the behavior thought to be caused by other factors. In each year, respondents were asked for whom they voted in the presidential election that had recently passed.[5] Vote choice is coded as a dichotomous variable with respondents reporting a vote for the Democratic ticket coded 1 and a vote for the Republican ticket coded 0.[3] Given the dichotomous nature of the dependent variable, logistic regression analyses were performed. The key independent variables of interest – the factors thought to cause vote choice – are the feeling thermometers for the presidential and vice presidential candidates in each year. For each candidate, respondents were asked to rate him/her on a scale from 0 to 100, with 100 indicating that the respondent felt "warm" toward that person, a score of 0 meaning that the respondent felt "cold" toward that person, and a score of 50 suggesting that the respondent did not feel either.[7]

As Table 2.1 illustrates, voters tend to be lukewarm about most candidates, rating most of them at about 50 on the 100 point scale. Still, there is great variation in these ratings with some candidates more warmly embraced by the electorate than others. The public most warmly rated Jimmy Carter's 1976 candidacy, rating him about seven points above the average for all other presidential candidates since the 1970s. In contrast, the public largely shunned Dan Quayle's 1992 reelection

Table 2.1: Mean Candidate Thermometer Ratings, 1972-2008

	1972	1976	1980	1984	1988	1992	1996	2000	2004	2008	Mean, 1972-2008
Democratic Presidential Candidate Rating	48.90 (29.04)	62.37 (25.91)	56.33 (27.04)	57.15 (25.31)	56.50 (26.29)	55.95 (24.19)	59.04 (29.17)	57.40 (25.38)	52.96 (26.15)	55.83 (35.32)	**56.24**
Republican Presidential Candidate Rating	50.01 (25.36)	53.21 (20.14)	54.14 (20.34)	57.18 (25.55)	53.07 (21.88)	57.19 (22.76)	58.02 (24.19)	57.35 (21.36)	55.36 (24.16)	55.87 (31.18)	**55.14**
Democratic Vice Presidential Candidate Rating	65.50 (26.47)	60.74 (23.46)	55.96 (25.21)	60.85 (28.26)	60.22 (27.23)	52.30 (26.11)	51.71 (23.34)	56.00 (24.62)	54.51 (32.97)	54.43 (31.29)	**57.22**
Republican Vice Presidential Candidate Rating	54.29 (27.09)	51.37 (20.35)	54.87 (18.39)	55.35 (21.57)	45.79 (24.14)	42.26 (26.11)	56.77 (20.02)	56.30 (22.03)	49.37 (28.27)	49.40 (35.34)	**51.58**

Notes: Cell entries are mean and standard deviations (in parentheses) of the presidential and vice-presidential thermometer ratings taken from the American National Election Studies (ANES Cumulative Data File).

bid, rating him a chilly twelve degrees below the VP average. Further, as others have suggested (Cohen 2001a), there is evidence that voters separate their assessments of presidential and vice presidential candidates. While the public turned a cold shoulder to George McGovern in 1972 (offering him the lowest average rating of all presidential candidates since 1972), voters embraced his running mate, Sargent Shriver, with the warmest rating of all VP candidates in this period.[8]

These presidential candidate ratings are included as predictors of vote choice, with the expectation that higher ratings of the Democratic presidential candidate will be positively related and higher ratings of the Republican presidential candidate will be negatively related to a vote for the Democratic ticket. Ratings for the Democratic and Republican VP candidates are included as predictors of vote choice as well, but they are not expected to be as consistently important as ratings of the presidential candidates. Still, when they are significant predictors of vote choice, I expect ratings of the Democratic vice presidential candidates to exhibit positive relationships with Democratic vote choice and Republican VP candidate ratings to exhibit negative relationships.

In addition to these thermometer ratings of candidates, control variables for key socio-demographic and attitudinal characteristics known to affect vote choice are included as well. Respondents' gender, age, race, and education level are included as controls with the expectation that women, younger respondents, minorities, and the less educated will be more likely to support Democratic presidential tickets.[9] Similarly, controls for respondents' self-reported partisanship and ideology are included with the expectation that Republicans and Conservatives will be less likely to support Democratic presidential tickets and Democrats and Liberals will be more likely to do so. Finally, given the long history of research into the importance of the economy in presidential elections, retrospective evaluations of the national economic situation are included in the model as well.[10] (See Appendix A for question wording and coding of all variables.)

To gauge the nature of the relationship between feelings about vice presidential candidates and vote choice, I perform a series of multivariate regression analyses. Table 2.2 presents the results from these analyses. The cell entries include regression coefficients, which can be interpreted in a straightforward manner. A positive coefficient indicates that more positive feelings about the candidate are associated with a higher likelihood of voting for the Democratic ticket, and a negative coefficient indicates that more positive feelings about the candidate are associated with a lower likelihood of voting for the Dem-

Table 2.2: Effect of Feelings about Candidates on Vote Choice, 1972-2008

	1972-2008	1972	1976	1980	1984	1988	1992	1996	2000	2004	2008
Democratic Presidential Candidate Rating	0.075 ** (0.003)	0.057 ** (0.006)	0.085 ** (0.009)	0.080 ** (0.011)	0.053 ** (0.009)	0.084 ** (0.010)	0.091 ** (0.011)	0.093 ** (0.013)	0.047 * (0.011)	0.057 * (0.006)	0.117 ** (0.014)
Republican Presidential Candidate Rating	-0.070 ** (0.003)	-0.058 ** (0.006)	-0.058 ** (0.009)	-0.070 ** (0.010)	-0.098 ** (0.010)	-0.085 ** (0.011)	-0.080 ** (0.011)	-0.075 ** (0.013)	-0.055 * (0.012)	-0.072 ** (0.005)	-0.084 ** (0.014)
Democratic Vice Presidential Candidate Rating	0.021 ** (0.003)	0.016 ** (0.006)	0.027 ** (0.010)	0.025 * (0.011)	0.029 ** (0.008)	0.010 (0.008)	0.034 ** (0.010)	0.012 (0.011)	0.029 * (0.012)	-0.001 (0.006)	0.040 ** (0.012)
Republican Vice Presidential Candidate Rating	-0.022 ** (0.003)	-0.012 * (0.005)	-0.030 ** (0.009)	-0.031 ** (0.010)	-0.005 (0.009)	-0.022 ** (0.008)	-0.023 ** (0.009)	-0.019 (0.013)	-0.034 ** (0.011)	-0.002 (0.005)	-0.031 ** (0.010)
Economic Evaluations	----	----	----	-0.361 (0.346)	-0.126 (0.149)	-0.576 ** (0.208)	-0.207 (0.312)	-0.005 (0.181)	-0.313 (0.185)	-0.528 ** (0.137)	-0.053 (0.717)
Female	-0.210 ** (0.097)	0.234 (0.203)	-0.509 * (0.254)	0.097 (0.289)	0.018 (0.257)	-0.193 (0.311)	-0.328 (0.317)	-0.392 (0.344)	-0.323 * (0.344)	-0.308 (0.201)	-0.010 (0.373)
Age	-0.002 (0.003)	-0.015 * (0.007)	0.007 (0.008)	0.003 (0.009)	0.010 (0.009)	0.001 (0.009)	-0.008 (0.009)	0.006 (0.010)	-0.009 (0.011)	-0.008 (0.006)	-0.038 ** (0.013)
Minority	0.772 ** (0.143)	0.737 * (0.337)	0.099 (0.467)	1.436 ** (0.513)	0.939 ** (0.345)	1.383 ** (0.484)	0.240 (0.411)	1.119 * (0.492)	1.171 * (0.481)	1.408 ** (0.281)	0.587 (0.398)
Education	-0.028 * (0.014)	-0.168 (0.125)	-0.098 (0.143)	-0.030 (0.182)	-0.066 (0.157)	0.010 (0.174)	-0.304 (0.187)	-0.439 * (0.214)	-0.456 (0.215)	-0.387 ** (0.120)	-0.037 (0.079)
Democrat	0.936 ** (0.147)	0.755 * (0.318)	0.711 * (0.352)	1.556 ** (0.499)	1.302 ** (0.385)	0.918 * (0.472)	1.486 ** (0.446)	2.409 ** (0.610)	0.706 (0.569)	0.826 * (0.320)	1.352 * (0.540)
Republican	-0.592 ** (0.158)	-0.460 (0.374)	-1.163 ** (0.382)	0.015 (0.562)	-0.210 (0.447)	-0.421 (0.489)	-0.348 (0.439)	0.596 (0.583)	-0.717 (0.569)	-0.660 (0.338)	-0.371 (0.561)
Liberal	0.457 ** (0.129)	0.662 * (0.265)	0.083 (0.356)	0.712 (0.412)	0.651 * (0.337)	0.517 (0.472)	0.998 (0.474)	0.425 (0.564)	0.432 (0.703)	0.538 (0.338)	-0.024 (0.491)
Conservative	-0.396 ** (0.112)	-0.104 (0.253)	-0.777 ** (0.298)	0.259 (0.347)	0.040 (0.313)	-0.516 (0.343)	-0.864 * (0.352)	-0.335 (0.377)	0.037 (0.653)	0.055 (0.318)	-1.187 ** (0.447)
Constant	-0.521 (0.302)	0.055 (0.736)	-1.150 (0.964)	-1.830 (1.207)	0.114 (1.000)	1.218 (1.067)	0.378 (1.201)	-0.654 (1.252)	2.657 (1.434)	3.206 ** (0.771)	-1.137 (2.218)
Number of Cases	9933	1366	957	723	1250	859	1165	904	783	879	1047
Pseudo R-Squared	0.737	0.628	0.661	0.675	0.748	0.743	0.803	0.794	0.768	0.799	0.852

Notes: Dependent variable is vote for Democratic ticket (1 = vote for Democratic ticket; 0 = vote for Republican ticket). Cell entries are unstandardized logit regression coefficient and standard errors (in parentheses). **p<0.00, *p<0.05, two-tailed.

ocratic candidate. The larger the absolute value of the coefficient, the more impact feelings have on vote choice.

The regression results confirm the relationship that feelings about presidential and vice presidential candidates have on vote choice. As the first column of this table reveals, more favorable ratings of the Democratic presidential candidate are positively related to voting for the Democratic ticket, while more favorable ratings of the Republican presidential candidate are negatively related to voting for the Democratic ticket. Similarly, feelings about VP candidates prove to be important to vote choice, though, as indicated by the smaller coefficient, they exhibit a somewhat smaller impact. When we look to the yearly results, it becomes clear that feelings about vice presidential candidates affect vote choice less consistently. Feelings about the presidential candidates played a role in shaping vote choice in every election. When it comes to VP candidates, however, the pattern is less clear. In some elections, feelings about both VP candidates matter; in others, only feelings about one ticket's VP candidate exhibit an impact on vote choice. Still, in others, feelings about neither VP candidate appear to have an effect on vote choice. Importantly, however, in elections when feelings about vice presidential candidates exhibit an impact on vote choice, the effects are in the expected direction. More favorable ratings of the Democratic vice presidential candidate are positively related to voting for the Democratic ticket, while more favorable ratings of the Republican presidential candidate are negatively related to voting for the Democratic ticket.

To better illustrate how much impact feelings about vice presidential candidates have on vote choice in each election, I calculated the magnitude of effect that feelings about VP candidates would have on the likelihood of voting for the Democratic ticket in each election. To produce these impact scores, I first predicted the baseline probability of voting for the Democratic ticket in each year by setting the thermometer ratings to the annual means reported in Table 2.1 and all control variables to their annual modal values, except age (which was set to the mean). For example, in 2008, the typical voter was a 47-year-old Anglo female with about 13 years of formal education who reported being a moderate Democrat and felt that national economic conditions over the past year had remained about the same.

I then predicted the probability of this typical voter casting a ballot for the Democratic ticket with a 25 point thermometer rating increase in each candidate rating in each year (i.e., I held all control variables constant but increased one candidate thermometer by 25 points). A 25 point increase was selected because the typical standard deviation of thermometer ratings for presidential and vice presidential candidates over the entire 1972-2008 period is 24.7 points. Thus, a change of 25 points on the 100 point scale represents the "typical" deviation in thermometer ratings across the period.

Table 2.3 presents the change in probability of voting for the Democratic ticket for a 25 point thermometer rating increase in each candidate rating in each year, while holding all other variables constant.[11] For instance in 2008, holding all else constant, an increase of 25 points in Biden's thermometer rating increases the probability of the typical voter supporting the Obama-Biden ticket by about 0.07 (or about 7%), and a similar increase in Palin's thermometer rating decreases the probability of a Democratic vote by about 0.11 (or about 11%). Thus, Palin exhibits a stronger impact on voters than Biden.

Historically, feelings about presidential candidates have exhibited a stronger and more consistent impact on vote choice than feelings about vice presidential candidates. While feelings about presidential candidates are associated with vote choice in every election since 1972, feelings about only seven Democratic and seven Republican VP candidates show a significant relationship with vote choice (see Table 2 1). Further, feelings about presidential candidates generally have a much stronger substantive impact on vote choice than feelings about vice presidential candidates. A 25 point increase in the typical Democratic presidential candidate's rating increases the average voter's chance of supporting that ticket by about 33% (+0.327), while the same increase in his Republican counterpart's rating decreases this voter's support of the Democratic ticket by almost 36% (-0.361).[12] The impact of VP candidates is comparatively small, with a 25 point improvement in the typical Democratic vice presidential candidate's rating leading to about a 14% increase in the average voter's support of that ticket and the same increase in the Republican VP candidate's rating decreasing support for that ticket by about 12%.

Isolating the Impact of VP Candidates Over Time

To explore the possibility that feelings about vice presidential candidates are more important to Independent voters than to partisan ones, I performed separate analyses for subsamples of partisans and Independents. As noted in Appendix A, Independents are "pure Independents," that is, those initially expressing no allegiance to either party nor reporting "leaning" toward either major party. Leaning partisans were coded the same as weak and strong partisans for purposes

Table 2.3: Substantive Impact of Candidate Ratings on Vote Choice, 1972-2008

	1972	1976	1980	1984	1988	1992	1996	2000	2004	2008	Mean, 1972-2008
Democratic Presidential Candidate Rating	0.325	0.297	0.455	0.303	0.327	0.307	0.342	0.342	0.280	0.295	**0.327**
Republican Presidential Candidate Rating	-0.289	-0.346	-0.246	-0.387	-0.445	-0.447	-0.413	-0.371	-0.263	-0.407	**-0.361**
Democratic Vice-Presidential Candidate Rating	0.099	0.136	0.147	0.180	0.061	0.166	0.072	0.276	0.177	0.073	**0.139**
Republican Vice-Presidential Candidate Rating	-0.073	-0.182	-0.142	-0.030	-0.138	-0.139	-0.120	-0.053	-0.185	-0.109	**-0.117**

Notes: Cell entries are the change in probability for a 25 point increase in the candidate rating, while holding all other variables at their means. These probabilities are calculated using the models presented in Table 2.2.

of this analysis. I first predicted baseline probabilities of voting for the Democratic ticket in each year for voters with three different profiles – the typical Democratic voter, the typical Republican voter, and the typical Independent voter. I did this by setting the thermometer ratings to the annual means reported in Table 2.1 and all control variables to their annual modal values, except age (which was set to the mean).[13] Based on these predicted probabilities, each voter was coded as either a baseline Democratic or Republican voter. Any voter with more than a 0.50 or higher probability of voting for the Democratic ticket was coded as a supporting the Democratic ticket, while those with a probability lower than 0.50 were coded as supporting the Republican ticket.

I then predicted an adjusted probability of supporting the Democratic ticket for each respondent by increasing the rating of the Democratic vice presidential candidate by 25 points, while holding all other variables at their baseline values. Based on these adjusted probabilities, I again coded each voter as either a Democratic or Republican ticket supporter (once again, those with adjusted probabilities of 0.50 or more were considered Democratic voters and those with probabilities less than 0.50 were considered Republican voters). I then compared each voter's baseline predicted party vote to his/her adjusted predicted party vote to determine whether the respondent's baseline predicted party vote and adjusted predicted party vote were different. Respondents whose baseline and predicted party votes differed were coded as being affected by the increased ratings of the Democratic VP candidate, while those whose baseline and predicted party votes were the same were coded as not being affected by the warmer rating of the Democratic vice presidential candidate. I then reset the Democratic rating to its mean and repeated this process for a 25 point improvement in the Republican VP candidates' ratings. Finally, I calculated the percentage of voters in each partisan subsample who were affected by changes in the vice presidential ratings.

These analyses provide a picture of the aggregate effect that vice presidential candidates had on the voting preferences of Democratic, Republican, and Independent voters. Among the partisan subsample, feelings about VP candidates prove to be largely insignificant. Because the baseline probability of voting for their own party's ticket is so high, the vote preferences of incredibly few partisans are affected when vice presidential candidate ratings are manipulated.[14] In fact, in any given year, the vote choices of less than one half of one percent of all partisans appear to be affected when ratings of VP candidates are increased by 25 points.

The picture is quite different among Independent voters, however. Among this subsample, feelings about VP candidates prove very important. Figure 2.1 illustrates the impact that a change in vice presidential ratings has on Independent voters in each election. As expected, when feelings about the Democratic vice presidential candidate increase, more Independent voters report favoring the Democratic ticket. Across the entire period, a 25 point boost in Democratic VP ratings draws approximately an additional 17% of Independents to support the ticket. Similarly, as feelings about Republican VP candidates were increased, fewer Independent voters report favoring the Democratic ticket. Since 1972, enhanced Republican vice presidential ratings appear to siphon off about 11% of the Independent vote from the Democrats. [15]

Figure 2.1: Percent of Independent Voters Affected by Increase in Vice Presidential Candidate Ratings, 1972-2008

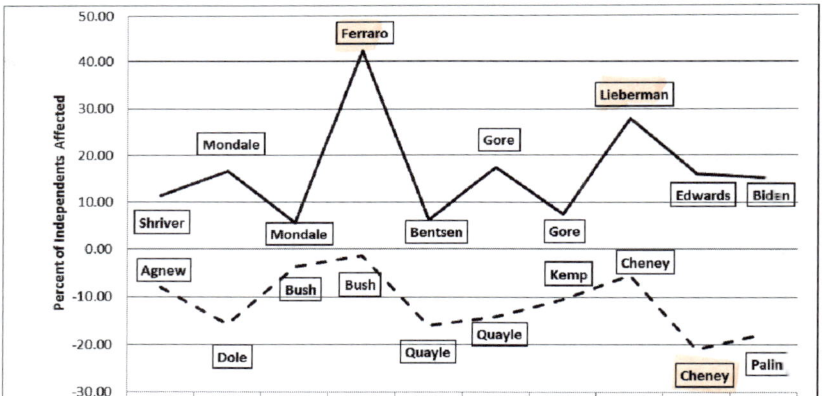

	1972	1976	1980	1984	1988	1992	1996	2000	2004	2008
—— Dem VP	11.40	16.50	5.60	42.20	6.30	17.30	7.50	27.80	15.90	15.20
– – Rep VP	-8.00	-15.60	-3.70	-1.38	-15.90	-14.10	-10.40	-5.30	-21.00	-17.70

Note: Vertical axis represents the change in percent of Independent voters expressing a preference for Democratic candidate when thermometer ratings of the VP candidate are increased by 25 points.

While some vice presidents have only minor electoral impacts, others prove to be highly influential among Independent voters. As a VP candidate, George H.W. Bush proved be the least influential vice presidential candidate in this era – swaying only about 3.7% of

Independents in his first bid and 1.4% of these voters in his re-election year. Two-time vice presidential candidates do not always remain inconsequential, however. While Dick Cheney's influence in the 2000 election was the third weakest of all VP candidates since 1970, his candidacy in the 2004 re-election campaign exhibited the third highest impact over the period. The groundbreaking 1984 candidacy of Geraldine Ferraro, the first woman to ever be nominated as a presidential running mate, represents the most influential VP candidacy since 1970. Feelings about Ferraro swayed the votes of more than 40% of the Independent electorate. Similarly, impressions of Jewish candidate Joe Lieberman played a role in the vote choice of nearly 28% of these voters. Sarah Palin's recent impact on almost 18% of Independent voters in the 2008 election rounds out the top four most influential vice presidential candidacies since the 1970s.

Summary

Despite strong arguments that vice presidential candidates should matter very little when it comes to voter decision making in presidential elections, there is evidence that sometimes feelings about the bottom of the ticket actually do affect voters' decisions about which ticket to support. Importantly, however, not all voters weigh their feelings about vice presidential candidates as heavily, and not all VP candidates matter to the same degree.

This chapter sought to determine if feelings about vice presidential candidates did indeed have an impact on voter decision making, and, if so, which voters would be most influenced by these feelings. The analyses presented here revealed that feelings about the bottom of the ticket impact the vote choices of those with no partisan allegiances more than those self-identifying as either Democrats or Republicans. Between 1972 and 2008, it was estimated that an average of about 17% of all Independent voters were persuaded to support the Democratic ticket because of more positive feelings about the VP candidate on that ticket, and about 11% of all Independent voters were swayed to support the Republican ticket because of improved feelings about the candidate on the bottom of that party's ticket.

This chapter further sought to examine the actual impact that vice presidential candidates of the past four decades have exhibited on vote choice. Using a newly developed measure of candidate impact, the analyses presented here illustrate that not all VP candidates matter to the same degree. Some candidates seem to matter to voters and others do not. Further, some candidates exhibit much stronger impacts than others.

The next chapter turns its attention to understanding why some vice presidential candidates mean more to voters than others. Given the theoretical importance of media coverage of VP candidates outlined in this chapter, I next explore the possibility that voters' feelings about a vice presidential candidate will affect their vote choices more when the media spends more time talking about that candidate.

Notes

[1] A search for (all versions of the) presidential and vice presidential candidates' names in the *New York Times* between Labor Day and election day of each presidential election year indicates that presidential candidates are mentioned in an average of 1,493 articles per election season while VP candidates garner 368 mentions in the same time period.

[2] Volumes 34(1): 8-83; 37(4): 733-767; 41(4):679-764

[3] The ANES data are available through the American National Election Studies on-line Data Center: http://www.electionstudies.org/.

[4] I focus on this time period for two key reasons. First, the year 1972 marks the first election year both parties fully adopted the use of the primary/caucus election system for nominations. Many point out that this shift led to a number of important changes in the electoral politics of presidential elections (see e.g., Hiller and Kriner 2008) including a tendency to downplay ticket balancing concerns in favor of governing concerns. The second reason to focus on this time span is more practical and involves access to appropriate data. The analyses conducted in this book require a dataset providing individual-level measures on a range of attitudes relevant to vote choice. Further, these data needed to provide consistent measurement of these attitudes over a long period of time. The American National Election Studies data offer consistent survey measures of the variables relevant to this study over the period examined here, but measures are less consistently available before 1972.

[5] Only respondents reporting a vote in the presidential election on the post-election NES survey were included in this analysis. When all respondents' pre-election vote intention is substituted for vote choice, the results remain statistically and substantively consistent with those presented here.

[6] Respondents reporting a vote for a third-party candidate are excluded from analysis.

[7] Following Wattenberg (1995) thermometer ratings were taken from the pre-election phase of the NES survey data. Since the pre-election survey is typically conducted in September and early October, using the pre-election thermometers allows me to estimate a baseline VP impact before the bulk of the campaign has unfolded. Further, the pre- and post-election thermometers are highly correlated and when the post-election measures are substituted for the pre-election measures in the multivariate models described here the results are statistically and substantively unchanged. Since post-election thermometer ratings were not consistently collected, the models relying on these measures suffer from a large number of missing cases.

[8] Of course, we must remember that Shriver's popularity with the public may be partially a result of his comparison to the failed candidacy of Thomas Eagleton (see e.g., Hiller and Kriner 2008).

[9] The race variable utilized is a dichotomous one indicating whether the respondent reports being a minority. The analyses were also conducted using separate dichotomous variables for African-American and Latino respondents. The results for all years were unchanged by this substitution, but the African-American variable causes severe collinearity problems in the 2008 model. Consequently, the "minority" dummy variable is utilized in all models.

[10] Since the economic evaluation variable was unavailable in the 1972 and 1976 datasets, this variable is excluded from the analyses for those years. Results from the 1972 and 1976 models substituting egocentric retrospective economic evaluations for sociotropic ones yields the same substantive results, but with far fewer cases. Sociotropic prospective, as well as egocentric prospective and retrospective economic evaluations were tested in the models for all years. The substantive results of the independent variables remain the same, but the alternate economic evaluation variables do not perform as well.

[11] A 25 point increase was selected because the typical standard deviation of thermometer ratings for presidential and VP candidates over the entire 1972-2008 period is 24.7 points. Thus, a change of 25 points on the 100 point scale represents the "typical" deviation in thermometer ratings across the period.

[12] Obama's low substantive impact compared to previous Democratic presidential candidates results from the much higher baseline probability the average voter had of supporting him. While the average voter had about a 0.507 chance of supporting previous Democratic presidential candidates, the typical 2008 voter exhibited about a 0.698 chance of supporting him, due largely to his higher than average thermometer rating.

[13] For these analyses control variables were set to their intra-party mode/mean. Republican identifiers were more likely to be older, Anglo, male, slightly more educated, and more conservative than Democratic and Independent identifiers. Similarly, Democratic and Independent identifiers differed in their profiles as well. Consequently, the modal/mean values of these control variables for Republican, Democratic and Independent identifiers were set to different values.

[14] The probability of supporting the Democratic Ticket among Democratic and Democratic leaning voters over the entire 1972-2008 period averages 0.98, and the probability of Republican and Republican leaning voters supporting the Republican ticket averages 0.99. It is important to remember that these probabilities are based on different "typical" voters. That is, the typical Democrat is younger, more likely to be female and non-Anglo, and marginally less educated than the typical Republican voter. Consequently, the value of the control variables is serving to increase these estimated probabilities.

[15] I replicated this analysis for each of the presidential candidates as well. As expected, the impact of feelings about presidential candidates was much greater than that of VP candidates, but was also primarily confined to the nonpartisan subsample. Among this subsample, more positive ratings of the Democratic presidential candidate attract an average of about 36% of Independent voters to their ticket across the 1972-2008 period, and enhanced Republican presidential candidate ratings detract about 28% of voters from the Democratic ticket.

3

How the Amount of Media Coverage Matters

The previous chapter illustrated how some vice presidential candidates have affected voter decision making more than others. This chapter seeks to understand why this is the case, and it looks for an answer in the growing importance of the media in American campaigns. Is it the case that second fiddles in the media spotlight steal the show? Since voters pay attention to candidates they hear more about, it seems likely that candidates receiving more media coverage should have a greater impact on voter decision making. When voters know more about vice presidential candidates, their feelings toward these candidates are more likely to shape their ultimate vote choices. This chapter investigates the question of whether candidates receiving more media coverage impact vote choice more.

After reviewing the importance of media coverage in presidential campaigns, I construct measures capturing the volume and intensity of media coverage received by vice presidential candidates; and I illustrate how some vice presidential candidates receive far more (and more intense), coverage than others. I next perform a series of statistical tests that confirm the expected relationship between media coverage and vice presidential impact on voters. Second fiddles who receive more media coverage do indeed impact voters more strongly.

Voter Decision Making in Presidential Elections

When it comes to making decisions in presidential elections, a variety of long term pre-existing attitudes and more short term pressing considerations sway voters. Voting scholars have long acknowledged the important and impressive impact that long-term influences such as partisanship and social group memberships have on individual-level vote choice (see e.g., Berelson, Lazarsfeld, and McPhee 1954; Campbell, et al 1960). In fact, research has shown that more than half of voters support the same candidate on Election Day as they did at the onset of the campaign and only a very small portion (about 5-8%) of all voters change their vote intention between mid-summer and November (Lazarsfeld, Berelson, and Gaudet 1944). Accordingly, a number of studies suggest that presidential campaigns do little to change voters' minds (Finkel 1993; Markus 1982; Miller and Shanks 1982; Patterson 1980).

Even short-term considerations emerging closer to the campaign period, such as perceptions of economic conditions and presidential popularity, are argued to exert relatively stable influences over the course of the campaign (Markus 1988; Lewis-Beck 1989). Further, some suggest that attention to such matters during the campaign only serves to reinforce pre-existing vote choice, not change it. "Instead of pushing citizens around, exposure to mass communication merely reinforces preexisting attitudes" (McDonald and Lentz 2009: 394; see also Ansolabehere and Iyengar 1995; Berelson, Lazarsfeld, and McPhee 1954; Finkel 1993; Klapper 1960; Lazarsfeld, Berelson, and Gaudet 1948; Markus 1988; McGuire 1986). In fact, Finkel (1993) found that using a voter's race and pre-campaign partisan identification along with evaluations of the incumbent president's performance resulted in a model accounting for over 80% of the votes in the 1980 election, and adding voter perceptions of candidate competence and personal integrity to the model only boosted its predictive power to 84%. Thus, many conclude that, no matter what new information the campaign produces, its main effect is to return voters to their original vote choice.

While this "minimal effects" view of campaigns initially garnered much support, researchers soon came to realize that campaigns operate in a more complicated way than first imagined. Rather than expecting a direct link between campaign exposure and vote choice, researchers have suggested that exposure to campaign messages subtly alters key impressions and attitudes that subsequently affect vote choice. For instance, media coverage of presidential campaigns has been shown to affect partisanship (Alsop and Weisbert 1988; Markus 1982, 1988) and bring about changes in short-term evaluations of presidential approval (West 1991), both important predictors of vote choice. Press endorsements of candidates can lead to more favorable candidate evaluations (Kahn and Kenney 2002), which, in turn, ultimately influence vote choice (Coombs 1981; Erikson 1976; Krebs 1998; McDonald and Lentz 2009; Robinson 1974). More generally, the overall content of the media messages also affects voters, with the editorial "slant" of media affecting candidate preference (Dalton, Beck, and Huckfeldt 1998; Druckman and Parkin 2005; Noelle-Neumann 1984; Zaller 1996). Barker (1999, 2002), for instance, illustrated that listening to Rush Limbaugh broadcasts increased voter preference for the Republican party independent of a litany of other important considerations. Further, there is evidence that the public responds to campaign events (Holbrook 1996; Hillygus 2005), especially television advertising (Huber and Arceneaux 2007; Johnston, Hagen, and Jamieson 2004), that the nature of the issues discussed during the campaign can affect vote choice (Clinton and Lapinski 2004; Carsey 2000; Gabel and Scheve 2007; Popkin 1991; Simon 2002; Zaller 1992), and that campaign intensity relates to voter turnout and statewide candidate preferences and electoral college outcomes (Holbrook and McClurg 2005; Shaw 1999). This wealth of evidence leaves little doubt that campaign media coverage can indeed "alter the outcome of elections and . . . influence the decisions of individual voters" (Peterson 2009: 446; see also Campbell 2000; Gelman and King 1993; Holbrook 1994,1996; Shaw 1999; Stimson 2004; Wlezien and Erikson 2002). So whether buttressing preexisting attitudes or shaping new ones, the scholarly consensus is that campaign information does indeed affect the outcome of elections (Brady, Johnston, and Sides 2006; Wlezien and Erikson 2002), and many have pointed to the importance of the media in explaining these effects (see e.g., Finkel 1993: 18).

Shining the Media Spotlight on Presidential Elections

The link between election news coverage and electoral behavior has been so well established that some have argued that "news media messages can be one of the most powerful influences on voting" (McDonald and Lentz 2009: 405). To explain the multitude of media effects that researchers have uncovered, many turn to the theory of media priming (e.g., Iyengar and Kinder 1987). "The idea of priming builds on the argument that the media's greatest impact is not in changing people's minds, but in influencing what issues citizens consider when making political assessments" (Kelleher and Wolack 2006: 194). By focusing on some elements of the campaign more than others, the media primes voters to weigh those elements more heavily in their candidate evaluations and vote choice. It is important to remember that priming represents a very different mechanism than persuasion (Miller and Krosnick 1996: 81). While persuasion involves changing the voter's substantive evaluation of the candidate, priming alters the criteria by which the voter rates the candidate. The media, it is argued, do not tell voters *how* to feel about the candidates, but rather tell them *what* to consider when they think about how they feel about the candidate. So, for instance, when the media emphasized the Persian Gulf War in the 1992 election, voters were more likely to base their presidential evaluations on President Bush's handling of the war than on other issues (Krosnick and Brannon 1993).

Evidence of priming effects abound, with studies conducted inside the laboratory and in the field documenting the numerous ways the news media influence the criteria voters use to judge political candidates and officeholders (see e.g., Iyengar and Kinder, 1987; Krosnick and Kinder, 1990). The media's focus on national economic conditions during the 1992 campaign, for instance, caused voters to rate incumbent President George H.W. Bush more negatively and, thus, decreased the likelihood of their casting a ballot for him in the election (Hetherington 1996). Similarly, Krosnick and Brannon (1993) showed how the media's attention to the Gulf War primed voters to evaluate the candidates in terms of their handling of the war. Evaluations of President Clinton were shown to be more greatly affected by considerations of his stances on abortion and the Family Medical Leave Act when potential voters were more heavily exposed to information about these issues (McGraw and Ling 2003). Similarly, voters can be primed to consider certain candidate traits more heavily than others. When key candidate traits such as integrity, leadership, and empathy are more heavily emphasized in campaigns, voters allow their perceptions of these traits to more strongly affect their vote choices (see e.g., Druckman 2004; Druckman and Holmes 204; Funk 1999; Jacobs and Shapiro 1994; McGraw and Ling 2003; Mendelsohn 1996).

Priming effects such as these likely apply to vice presidential candidates as well. In the same way that media concentration on a war, economic conditions, or a candidate's personal traits leads voters to more heavily weigh these factors when casting a ballot, heightened media coverage of vice presidential candidates likely causes voters to consider their impressions of those candidates more seriously when casting a ballot. When the media focuses on a vice presidential candidate more intensely, voters will know more about that candidate and be more likely to consider their feelings about the candidate when making a vote decision.

Some Voters Notice the Light More

Though the media can prime voters to consider some campaign elements more than others, not all voters will be equally affected. The strength of the priming effect depends largely on two key elements – the overall volume of media coverage focusing on a particular campaign element to which the voter is exposed and the openness of the voter to the information received (Zaller 1987). Many argue that as media coverage of an issue (or trait) increases, voters will rely more on their evaluations of that issue/trait when evaluating candidates and making their vote choice (e.g., Hetherington 1996; Malhotra and Krosnick 2007; Stoker 1993). "The more attention the news pays to a particular domain-the more frequently it is primed-the more citizens will, according to the theory, incorporate what they know about that domain into their overall judgment of the president" (Krosnick and Kinder 1990: 500).

At the same time, it is important to remember that some media consumers will be more open to the messages they receive than others. Since media messages related to political actors and events tend to carry partisan and ideological information, we must consider the way these messages affect voters of differing partisan attachments (McGuire 1968; Zaller 1987). Media messages are much less likely to affect partisan voters than those with no pre-existing partisan ties. While voters expressing loyalties to either the Democrat or Republican Party remain open to media messages favorable to their party's own candidates, they largely ignore messages portraying their candidate in a negative way or the opposing party's candidate in a positive manner (see e.g., Bartels 2002; Campbell, et al 1960; Taber and Lodge 2006; Zaller 1992). In contrast, media messages of all sorts are more likely to reach, and thus potentially impact, non-partisan voters. With no standing ties to either party, these voters are more likely to enter the campaign with no preconceived notions about the candidates (Hillygus and Shields 2008: 25) and readily receive both positive and negative information about candidates from both parties (see e.g., Zaller 1992).

Given the varied impact that media coverage is likely to have on partisans and non-partisans, it is reasonable to expect priming effects to be strongest among voters who call themselves Independents. Since non-partisan voters tend to make their ultimate vote choices much later in the campaign than partisan voters (Campbell, et al 1960), they will experience higher levels of exposure to the media's coverage of the candidates and their campaigns. Also, since they have no prevailing vote choice, they will remain open to receiving messages about candidates of every partisan stripe. Therefore, the more the media discusses vice presidential candidates, the more evaluations of these candidates should affect the vote choice of Independent voters.

Measuring the Volume and Intensity of Media Coverage

Much of the research into media effects relies on survey respondents to report the content of the media to which they were exposed. While such studies have their strengths, the validity of such measures has been questioned. As Prior (2009a: 893) notes, "survey respondents are bad at telling us accurately about their media exposure." In fact, some research suggests that only about half of survey respondents are able to accurately recall a televised campaign ad they saw about half an hour earlier (Ansolabehere, Iyengar, and Simon 1999). The problematic nature of such measures leads some to question studies of media effects that rely on such self-reports (see e.g., Prior 2009b: 137).

Given the difficulty of using self-reports, I take a more objective measure of media content for the analyses presented here. To quantify the volume and intensity of media coverage received by candidates in presidential elections since 1970, I conducted a content analysis of press coverage of these elections. While a wide range of media coverage of presidential campaigns exists, I focus on coverage presented in the *New York Times* newspaper during the general election campaign season of each election year. While the *New York Times* may not represent the primary source of media information for most Americans, it is widely accepted as a "reasonable record of the total conduct of campaigns" (Lau and Pomper 2004: 134; see also Druckman 2004). Further, the *Times* has been shown to serve as an agenda setter for other media outlets (Bartels 1996; Cohen 2008; Comstock and Scharrer 2005: 180; Grossman and Kumar 1981), with more commonly consumed media (local newspapers and television news) echoing its content.[1] Thus, stories reported in the *Times* offer a valid and reliable proxy measure for total media coverage of campaigns, especially campaigns for national office. In fact, studies of media effects frequently employ *New York Times* content to investigate the media's influence in U.S. Senate (e.g., Ansolabehere, et al 1994; Franklin 1991; Lau and Pomper 2004) and Presidential (e.g., Holian 2004; Kelleher and Wolak 2006) races.

Measuring Volume of Media Coverage

I measure volume of media coverage by counting the number of *New York Times* stories referencing each major party candidate for president and vice president during the general election campaign season that runs between Labor Day and Election Day of each election year. To arrive at this count, I searched for stories containing each candidate's name in LexisNexis Academic's newspaper archive. Each candidate's name served as the search term, and searches were limited to the *New York Times* between Labor Day and Election Day of each election year.[2] In total, I identified 37,222 stories referencing major party candidates in presidential elections since 1970.

Table 3.1 illustrates the amount of media coverage received by each presidential and vice presidential candidate since 1970. In addition to the raw number of stories about each candidate, the table presents the percentage of each year's campaign stories received by each candidate. In 2008, for instance, Republican vice presidential candidate Sarah Palin received a little more than 21% of the media coverage of all four major party candidates in the general election, while Joe Biden received less than 8% of this coverage.

As we would expect, the media are consistently more enamored with presidential candidates than with those on the bottom of the ticket. Major party presidential candidates receive an average of about 82% of the campaign season media coverage across the period, leaving vice presidential candidates vying for the remaining 18% of candidate coverage. At the same time, there is evidence that some vice presidential candidates receive more than their share of the media's attention while others are relatively ignored. Comparing the amount of coverage received by each party's presidential and vice presidential candidates in each year shows that there are times when the media fixates more on the bottom of the ticket. For this comparison, I calculated the 'relative media coverage' of each vice presidential candidate as the ratio of vice presidential to presidential media coverage (using the raw story counts). Across the entire time period, the vice presidential candidates received a relative media coverage score of 0.22, indicating that those on the bottom of the ticket receive about one-fifth as much coverage as their running mates.[3]

Table 3.1 also offers evidence that some vice presidential candidates garner far more than their share of the media spotlight while others are resigned to the shadows. While Spiro Agnew only managed to capture about 6% of the amount of media coverage as running mate Richard Nixon in the 1972 election, Sarah Palin received more than 60% of the amount of coverage that John McCain did in 2008. In addition to the phenomenal level of coverage the media showered on Palin, the media also seemed to have been taken by the candidacies of Geraldine Ferraro, Dan Quayle, and Joe Lieberman. Ferraro received nearly half as much coverage as her Presidential running mate Walter Mondale, while Dan Quayle and Joe Lieberman received about one-third as much coverage as their respective running mates. Notably, candidates with unique characteristics tend to attract more media attention. Female candidates

Table 3.1: Volume of Media Coverage of Presidential and Vice Presidential Candidates, 1972-2008

	1972	1976	1980	1984	1988	1992	1996	2000	2004	2008
Democratic Presidential Candidate	1496 (32.00)	973 (41.69)	2331 (57.37)	1144 (25.71)	969 (36.90)	1308 (34.38)	1807 (52.77)	1437 (39.16)	1450 (28.92)	1340 (35.48)
Republican Presidential Candidate	2792 (59.72)	1120 (47.99)	1293 (31.82)	2298 (51.64)	1091 (41.55)	1817 (47.77)	1080 (31.54)	1520 (41.42)	2319 (46.25)	1348 (35.69)
Democratic Vice Presidential Candidate	213 (4.56)	119 (5.10)	198 (4.87)	541 (12.16)	231 (8.80)	340 (8.94)	269 (7.86)	421 (11.47)	253 (5.04)	281 (7.44)
Relative Media Coverage	0.14	0.12	0.08	0.47	0.24	0.26	0.15	0.29	0.18	0.21
Republican Vice Presidential Candidate	174 (3.72)	122 (5.23)	241 (5.93)	467 (10.49)	335 (12.76)	339 (8.91)	268 (7.83)	292 (7.96)	377 (7.52)	808 (21.39)
Relative Media Coverage	0.06	0.11	0.19	0.2	0.31	0.19	0.25	0.19	0.16	0.63

Notes: Cell entries are raw number of stories mentioning candidate and percent of election media coverage mentioning candidate (in parentheses). For vice presidential candidates, *relative media coverage* is the ratio of vice presidential to presidential media coverage (calculated with raw story count).

Geraldine Ferraro and Sarah Palin rank among the top four most covered vice presidential candidates of the past four decades, as does Joe Lieberman, who did not shy away from his Jewish heritage. All three of these candidates break the mold of the traditional Protestant, male vice presidential candidate.

Capturing Intensity of Media Coverage

To capture the intensity with which the media covers each candidate, I examined a random sample of all the articles written about candidates during presidential campaigns of the past four decades (see Appendix B for details on sampling and coding procedures). Each of the selected stories about vice presidential candidates was coded to indicate the amount of coverage of the candidate in the story. Stories offering "very little" coverage of the candidate scored a 1, those offering "medium" amount of coverage scored a 2, and those with "a lot" of coverage of the candidate scored a 3. Each candidate's mean coverage score was then calculated. Table 3.2 presents the media intensity scores for each presidential and vice presidential candidate since 1970.

   Table 3.2 reveals that the media treats candidates fairly even-handedly. On average, candidates receive a moderate amount of media intensity, scoring about 1.4 on the three point scale overall. Further, presidential and vice presidential candidates receive about the same degree of intense coverage. While presidential candidates average 1.37 on the intensity scale, vice presidential candidates score 1.42, on average.[4] Still, the media covers some candidates much more intensely than others. While the media most intensely covered John McCain's 2008 presidential bid (which scored an above average 1.51), they were far less interested in Ronald Reagan's re-election campaign in 1984 (which scored only 1.17). Intensity for the bottom of the ticket varied even more. Spiro Agnew's 1972 candidacy generated the lowest media intensity score (1.13) and Geraldine Ferraro's 1984 bid generated the highest (1.68).

Amount of Media Coverage and Vice Presidential Impact

So far the evidence has shown that some vice presidential candidates exhibit a larger impact on voter decision making than others and that the media covers some of those on the bottom of the ticket more (and more intensely) than others. But are these things related? To investigate whether vice presidential candidates receiving more (and more intense) media coverage do indeed influence voter behavior more, I examined

Table 3.2: Intensity of Media Coverage of Presidential and Vice Presidential Candidates, 1972-2008

	1972	1976	1980	1984	1988	1992	1996	2000	2004	2008
Democratic Presidential Candidate	1.45	1.31	1.39	1.35	1.29	1.45	1.45	1.42	1.40	1.43
Republican Presidential Candidate	1.24	1.25	1.30	1.17	1.46	1.25	1.44	1.46	1.43	1.51
Democratic Vice Presidential Candidate	1.46	1.42	1.52	1.68	1.45	1.46	1.48	1.41	1.59	1.58
Republican Vice Presidential Candidate	1.13	1.27	1.25	1.42	1.39	1.34	1.24	1.38	1.27	1.55

Notes: Cell entries are media intensity scores, calculated as the mean amount of coverage of the candidate in a sample of stories referencing the candidate. Amount of coverage measured as: 1 = 'very little coverage' of the candidate in the story; 2= 'medium' amount of coverage of the candidate in the story; 3 = 'a lot' of coverage of the candidate in the story.

the relationship between these factors. Since I only care about the overall impact that feelings about a vice presidential candidate exhibited on voters, not whether these feelings made voters more or less likely to support a particular candidate, I take the absolute value of the vice presidential impact measure developed in Chapter 2 (see Figure 2.1) as my dependent variable.

Volume of Media Coverage

Figure 3.1 illustrates the connection between the amount of media coverage received by vice presidential candidates and their impact on Independent voters. As expected, vice presidential candidates standing in the media spotlight affect vote choice among Independents much more strongly than those shunned by the media. As Figure 3.1 illustrates, vice presidential media coverage and the substantive impact of vice presidents on Independent voters are positively (and significantly) related.[5] The more media coverage a vice presidential candidate receives, the more impact that candidate has on vote choice. On the Democratic side, Geraldine Ferraro, who received about twice as much media coverage as the typical Democratic vice presidential candidate, exhibits an extremely strong impact on Independent voters. When feelings about Ferraro increase by 25 points, the vote choices of about 42% of Independent voters are persuaded to more favorably support her ticket. Similarly, feelings about Sarah Palin, who received the most media coverage of any vice presidential candidate, strongly influenced Independent voters. A 25 point improvement in Palin's ratings drew about an additional 18% of Independents to support her ticket.

While these bivariate findings are suggestive, the possibility remains that something other than media coverage accounts for the impact that vice presidential candidates have on Independent voters. Vice presidential candidates might have an impact in elections because of their style and performance on the campaign trail. At the same time, the factors that more generally affect presidential elections, such as economic conditions or the popularity of the incumbent party's president, might explain why some vice presidential candidates matter more than others.[6] When economic concerns are forefront in voters' minds, they are likely to pay less attention to other factors, including vice presidential candidates. Similarly, a very popular president may lead voters to discount their feelings about the other candidates in the race, especially those on the bottom of the ticket.

Figure 3.1: Volume of Media Coverage and Vice Presidential Impact on Independent Voters, 1972-2008

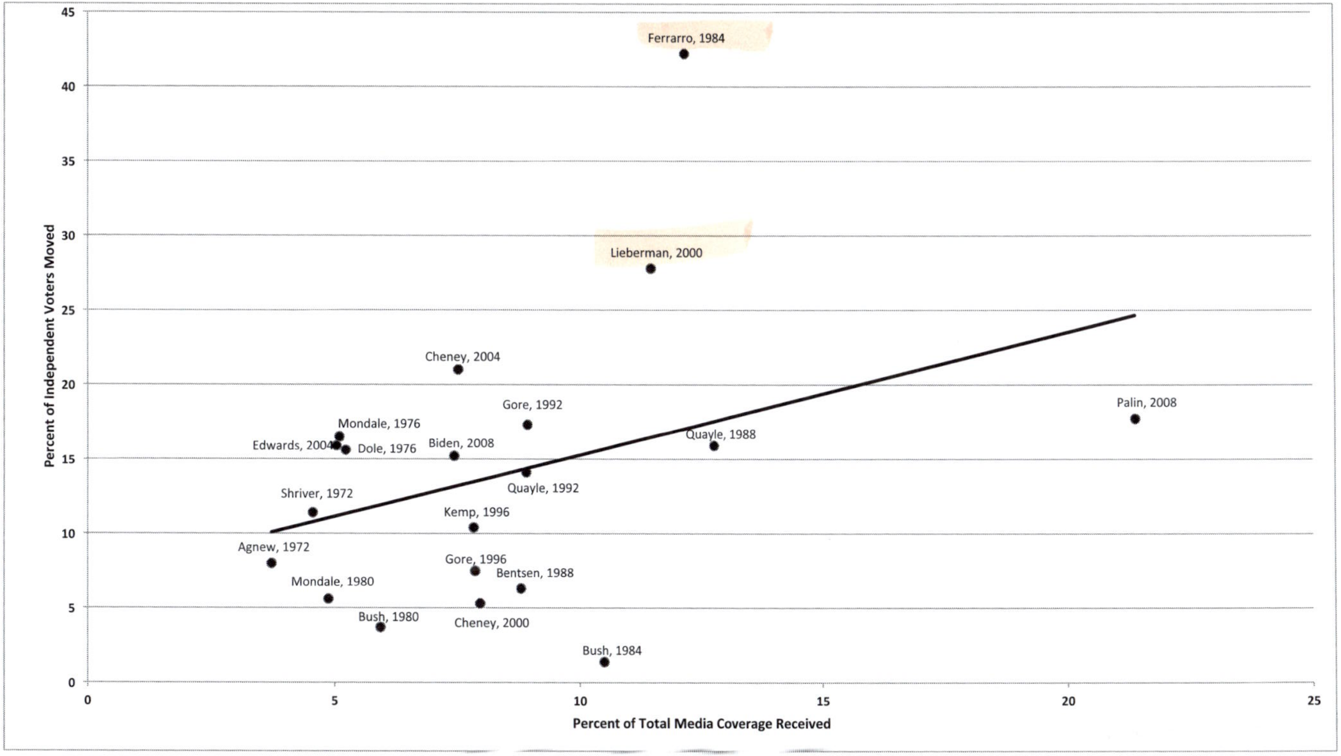

To account for these countervailing possibilities, I tested the relationship between the amount of media coverage and vice presidential impact while controlling for economic conditions and the incumbent president's popularity. I rely on Fair's (2009) economic model and take as the economic indicator the growth rate of real per capita GDP in the first three quarters of the election year. Since larger changes, either positive or negative, are expected to minimize the impact that vice presidential candidates have in an election, I use the absolute value of this variable. Larger economic changes, in either direction, are expected to lower vice presidential impact. I measure presidential popularity using the American National Election Studies pre-election measure of presidential approval. Higher percentages of public approval for the job the incumbent president is doing are expected to lessen the impact of the vice presidential candidates.

As the results in the first column of Table 3.3 illustrate, the relationship between amount of media coverage and vice presidential impact remains robust even after controlling for the state of the economy and the popularity of the incumbent president. Vice presidential candidates who receive more media attention affect Independent voters more than those who receive less. And the magnitude of this effect is impressive. For every additional percentage of media coverage that a vice presidential candidate garners, this model predicts that almost 1% more Independent voters will be affected.

Table 3.3: Amount of Media Coverage and Vice Presidential Impact, 1972-2008

	I.	II.	III.
Percent of Total Media Coverage Received	0.925 *	----	----
Coverage Intensity Score	----	29.967 *	----
Percent of Articles with Moderate Intensity Coverage	----	----	0.814 **
Presidential Approval	0.175	0.182	-0.046
Economic Conditions	0.247	-0.204	-1.084
Constant	-5.119	-38.670	7.559
Number of Cases	20	20	20
Adjusted R-squared	0.014	0.070	0.129

*Note: Cell entries are unstandardized OLS regression coefficients. Dependent variable is absolute value of "Percent of Independent Voters Affected" as reported in Figure 2.1. *p<0.10; **p<0.05 (two-tailed).*

In addition to the controls for economic condition and presidential popularity, I also tested a series of controls related to each vice president's presidential running mate. To investigate whether vice presidential candidates might impact voter choice more when voters have less information about the presidential candidate on the ticket, I replicated the models presented on Table 3.3 with the addition of a control variable measuring the overall amount of coverage received by each vice president's running mate (measured in the same manner that the volume of media coverage received by vice presidential candidates is measured). While the control variable for volume of media coverage of presidential candidates proves insignificant, the volume of media coverage received by vice presidential candidate remains statistically related to vice presidential impact.

I further examined whether vice presidential candidates have a greater impact when voters have doubts about their presidential running mates by including a number of controls for the negativity of the media coverage of presidential candidates.[7] Once again, the control variable proved to be unrelated to vice presidential impact, but the relationship between volume of vice presidential media coverage and vice presidential impact persisted. Next, I included measures for negative coverage of presidential candidates' physical appearance, race, sex, religion, marital status, children, and occupation.[8] The results remain the same; volume of vice presidential media coverage proves to be a predictor of vice presidential impact, but the control variables do not. I then included controls for negative coverage of the presidential candidates' intelligence, morality, leadership ability, and empathy, and the results were unchanged.[9] Finally, I included controls for whether presidential candidate made the voter feel angry, afraid, not hopeful, or not proud.[10] Once again, the controls proved insignificant while the volume of media coverage of vice presidential candidates proved to be a significant predictor of vice presidential impact.

Intensity of Media Coverage

While the preceding analysis revealed that voters' feelings about a vice presidential candidate affect their voting decision more when that candidate receives more media mentions, the candidates' share of campaign media coverage offers a somewhat crude measure of media coverage. While a candidate might be mentioned in a large number of media stories about the campaign, the candidate might not be the focus of these stories. If it is the case that voters are most affected by candidates they come to know best through the media, then we would expect those candidates who the media presents most fully to be most influential. To more closely examine the ways that amount of media coverage affects vice presidential candidate influence, I explored the content of the selected sample of vice presidential media coverage to see if more intense coverage of vice presidential candidates leads them to exert more impact on voters.

As Figure 3.2 illustrates, the more intense the media coverage of vice presidential candidates the more impact they have on voters.[11] While Spiro Agnew affected the vote choices of only about 8% of Independent voters, Ferraro's influence was felt by more than 42% of these voters. Further, it appears that moderate intensity coverage tends to affect more Independent voters than less, and even more, intense coverage. As column II of Table 3.3 reveals, this relationship withstands the addition of control variables for economic conditions and presidential popularity.[12] Vice presidential candidates receiving more intense media coverage affect the votes of more Independent voters. While the substantive impact suggested by the regression equation appears enormous (for every additional degree of intensity, nearly 30% more Independent voters are affected), it is important to remember that the standard deviation of this measure is only 0.12, suggesting a much smaller substantive impact. In fact, this model suggests a vice president receiving very intense media coverage (coverage that is 2 standard deviations above the mean), would affect the votes of about 7% more Independent voters than the typical vice presidential candidate.

Figure 3.3 investigates the relationship between the degree of moderate coverage that candidates receive and the impact they have on voters. As this figures shows, the higher the percentage of moderate intensity coverage received by a candidate, the higher the candidate's impact on Independent voters.[13] The same is not true for the percentage of low or high coverage, both of which prove to be unrelated to candidate impact.[14] This finding suggests a curvilinear relationship between media intensity and vice presidential influence.[15] Candidates receiving higher levels of moderately intense coverage tend to influence voter decision making, but those receiving either very high or very low intensity coverage have little impact on vote choice. Once again, Table 3.3 shows that this relationship remains even in the presence of control variables.[16] When measures of the economy and presidential approval are included, vice presidential candidates receiving more moderately intense coverage have a greater impact than those receiving less. In fact, this model suggests that for each additional percentage of moderately intense coverage a vice presidential candidate receives, the votes of about 0.81% more Independents will be affected.

Figure 3.2: Intensity of Media Coverage and Vice Presidential Impact on Independent Voters, 1972–2008

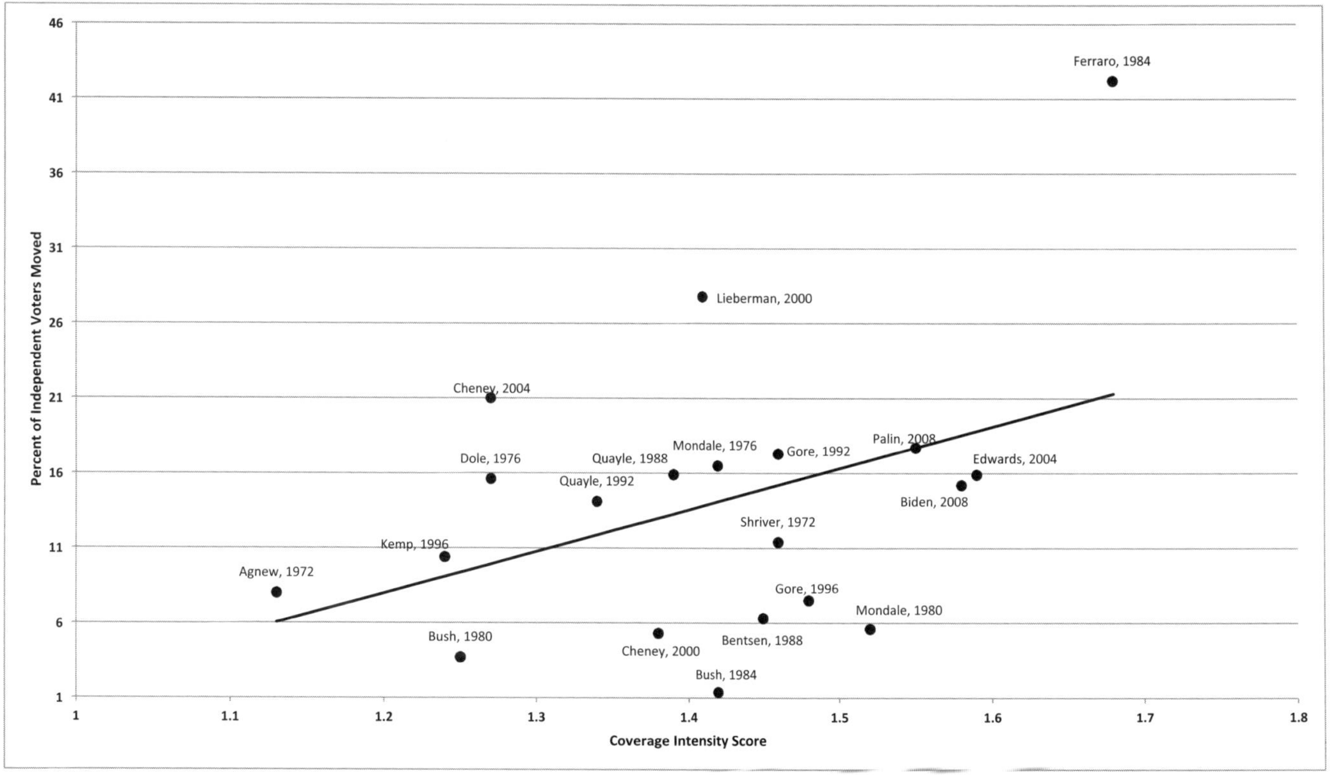

Figure 3.3: Moderate Intensity Media Coverage and Vice Presidential Impact on Independent Voters, 1972–2008

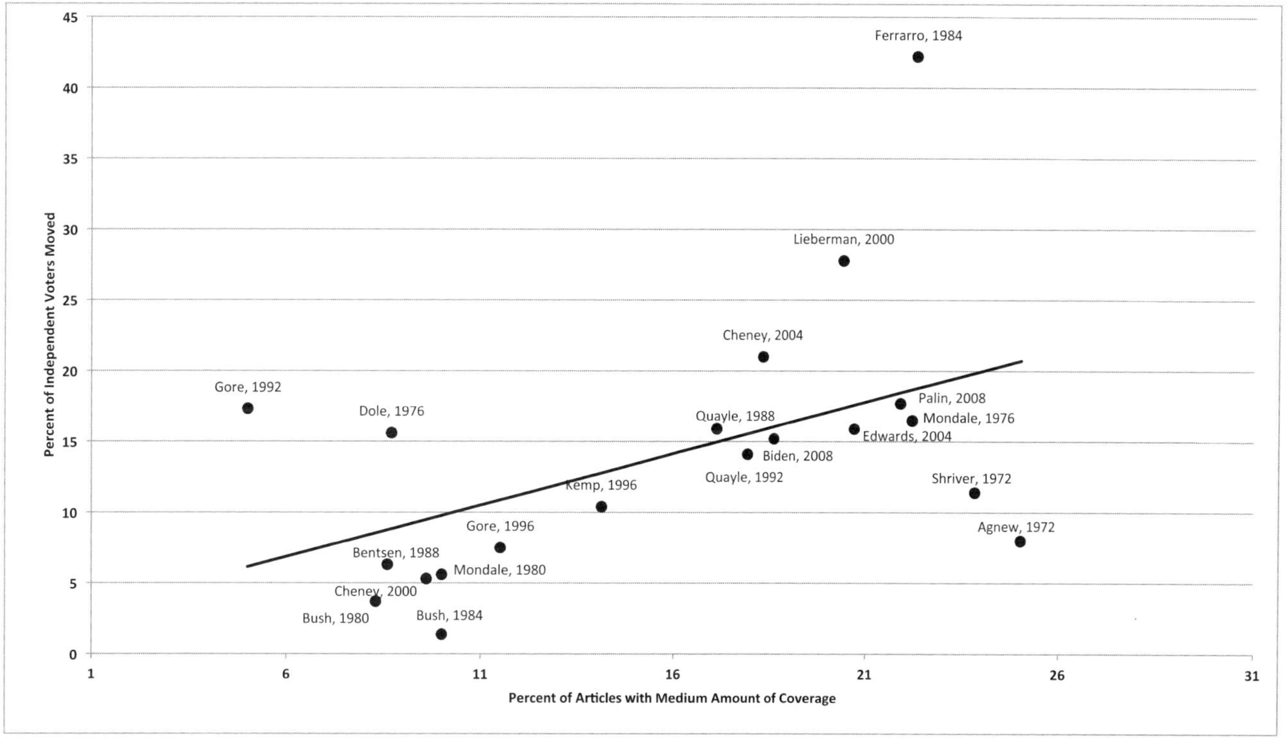

It certainly makes sense that low intensity coverage would offer voters little information on which to judge a vice presidential candidate and consequently lead evaluations of the candidate to play little role in vote choice. Though less intuitive, the finding that candidates who receive more intense coverage do not exert a larger impact on voters fits well with the similar findings from the field of social psychology showing that "the persuasive effect of communication first increases then wears out as repetition increases" (Cacioppo and Petty 1989: 10). Moderate levels of communication lead to better understanding of arguments (Cacioppo and Petty 1989), but these knowledge gains are lost as consumers become bored or satiated with the message with higher levels of repetition (Stang 1975). Similarly, it would appear that vice presidential candidates make the greatest impact when they receive moderate intensity coverage.

Summary

This chapter set out to understand why some vice presidential candidates matter more to voters than others. The analyses focused on the growing importance of the media in voter decision making and showed that voters are likely to pay more attention to candidates they hear more about. The chapter's findings suggest the amount and intensity of vice presidential candidate media coverage affects how much impact these candidates have on voters in the voting booth. When the media offers more stories referencing vice presidential candidates, voters allow their feelings toward these candidates to shape their ultimate vote choice. The findings also reveal that the sheer volume of media coverage is not all that matters. The intensity of that media coverage plays an important role as well. Candidates who receive more intense media coverage tend to affect voters more, and those receiving the highest levels of moderate intensity coverage appear to have the greatest impact. Taken together, these findings suggest that vice presidential candidates receiving a high volume of media coverage that does not overly concentrate on them will likely have the greatest impact on voters.

The next chapter further explores the importance of media content, asking whether the tone of vice presidential media coverage affects the impact that these candidates have on voters. After reviewing reasons why voters are likely to pay more attention to the negative information they receive from the media than to positive, I test to see if the media negativity aimed at vice presidential candidates leads voters to consider their feelings about these candidates more at election time.

Notes

[1] To further validate the use of the *Times* as my only source of media data, I recomputed the media volume and intensity scores presented in this chapter using content from the *Washington Post*. The measures based on *Times* data and those based on *Post* data correlated highly (media volume correlation = 0.993, p =0.000; media intensity correlation = 0.897, p=0.000), suggesting that the *Times* data are representative of the content of other media sources.

[2] Since it was possible, and in some cases likely, that such a search might return stories that contained reference to someone other than the candidate, but with the candidate's name. All stories returned in the search were scanned to ensure that the story was actually about the candidate of interest. Any stories found to be unrelated to the candidate were discarded.

[3] The relative coverage of Republican and Democratic vice presidential candidates is almost identical, with Republican vice presidential candidates averaging a relative media coverage score of 0.214 and Democrats averaging 0.229 across the time period.

[4] There also appear to be few partisan differences. Republican and Democratic presidential candidate have mean scores of 1.35 and 1.39, respectively. And Republican and Democratic vice presidential candidate average about 1.3 and 1.5, with the higher Democratic score driven almost entirely by the very high level of intensity surrounding Geraldine Ferraro.

[5] The Pearson's r correlation coefficient for the relationship between percent of all media coverage garnered by each vice presidential candidate and the percent of Independents affected by that candidate is 0.356 (p=0.035, two-tailed).

[6] In addition to these factors, it is possible that vice presidential candidates might have an impact in elections because of their style and performance on the campaign trail. As some have suggested, the vice presidential debates likely make an impression on voters (Kenski 2010; Romero 2004), and campaign appearances by candidates in a variety of races have been shown to affect the public (Althaus, Nardulli, and Shaw 2002; Herr 2002; Hill, Rodriquez, and Wooden 2010; Shaw and Gimpel 2012). Ideally, the multivariate models I present here would include measures of vice presidential candidate campaign appearances and debate performance. Unfortunately, such measures are not readily available. While some information about public perception of debate performance is accessible, it is not available for the entire time period under study here. Further, vice presidential debates were not held in 1972 or 1980, and including such a control would thus limit models containing an already small number of cases. Campaign appearance data on vice presidential candidates remains even more elusive, especially for the early years in this study.

[7] Measured in the same manner that vice presidential negativity is measured in Chapter 4.

[8] Measured in the same way that vice presidential coverage of these traits is measured in Chapter 5.

[9] These control variables were measured in the same manner that media coverage of these traits for vice presidential candidates were measured in Chapter 6.

[10] These variables were measured using the relevant NES survey items. The measure is the percent of respondents reporting that the presidential candidate makes them feel each way.

[11] The bivariate correlation for this relationship is 0.417 (p=0.067, two-tailed).

[12] This result also holds when controls for the presidential media coverage, traits, and characteristics discussed above are included.

[13] The bivariate correlation for this relationship is 0.488 (p=0.029, two-tailed).

[14] The bivariate correlation for the low intensity coverage is -0.306 (p=0.189, two-tailed) and the correlation for high intensity coverage is -0.142 (p=0.550, two tailed).

[15] A multivariate model that includes both the media intensity score and the squared media intensity score confirms this relationship. Both the base term and the squared term are statistically significant at p<0.10, with a positive coefficient for the base term and a negative one for the squared term.

[16] This result also holds when controls for the presidential media coverage, traits, and characteristics discussed above are included.

4

How the Negativity of Media Coverage Matters

In the previous chapter we saw that the volume and intensity of media coverage influence how much impact vice presidential candidates have on voters. When candidates receive more (and more intense) coverage voters are more likely to take their feelings about the candidates into account when casting a ballot. This chapter takes a closer look at the content of the coverage, particularly the importance of negative media coverage, and asks if second fiddles need flattering light to shine. Because voters fear possible costs associated with their vote more than they treasure possible benefits, voters tend to consider negative information about candidates more heavily than positive information. When the media bombards voters with negative information about a particular candidate, they will come to know more about that candidate and therefore take their feelings about him/her into account when voting. Consequently, we should expect candidates receiving more negative media coverage to have a greater impact on voters than those receiving more positive coverage.

I first review the reasons why voters are likely to attend to and learn from negative information about candidates more than from positive or neutral information. I next construct measures capturing the negativity of media coverage received by VP candidates and illustrate how some receive far more negative coverage than others. Finally, I perform a series of statistical analyses aimed at testing the expected relationship between negative media coverage and VP impact on voters. Contrary to expectations, media negativity does not increase voter impact for VPs in general, but negative media coverage of incumbent VP candidates during their first term greatly impacts voter behavior at reelection time.

Negative Information Means More Information

As the findings from the previous chapter illustrate, when the media more heavily covers vice presidential candidates, these candidates play a larger role in voter decision making. While few would question the importance of the media in modern politics, many argue that some types of information play a more important role than others. Negative information, in particular, has been cited as especially influential when it comes to shaping voter opinion and behavior. Though the public expresses distaste for negativity in campaigns, voters notice, process, and remember negative information more readily than positive information (Thurber, et al. 2000). Consequently, such information likely sticks with voters longer, making it more likely to affect the decisions they make in the voting booth.

Even when the sheer amount of positive information outweighs the negative, "[p]eople attend to negative stimuli and events in their environments much more quickly" (Kahn and Kenney 2004: 66; see also Fiske 1980; Hamilton and Zanna 1974; Johnson and Copeland 1989; Lau 1985). Some believe that negative information draws our attention because it stands out against our otherwise relatively positive lives (Lau 1982). Others argue that our desire to avoid costly mistakes drives our awareness of negative information. In general, people more actively seek to avoid costs rather than achieve gains (Kahn and Kenney 2000, 2004; Kanouse and Hanson 1972; Lau 1982, 1985; McGraw and Steenbergen 1997). In fact, our instinct to give "swift and seamless attention to negative information" is so ingrained that social psychologists have termed it "automatic vigilance" (Kahn and Kenney 2004: 66; Pratto and John 1991). Without even thinking about it, we pay attention to negative information more quickly. Since positive information does not alert us to the risks we seek to avoid, we react more slowly to it (Kahn and Kenney 2004). During campaigns, then, we can expect voters to more actively pay attention to information highlighting candidates' negative qualities than their positive attributes.

Not only do voters tend to notice negative information more, they tend to remember it better. A number of studies have shown that negative campaign ads are more memorable to survey respondents (Basil, Schooler, and Reeves 1991; Kahn and Kenney 2000; Lang 1991; Lau and Sigleman 2000; Newhagen and Reeves 1991; Roberts 1995; Sulfaro 1998), and that voters more quickly and accurately recall negative information (Newhagen and Reeves 1991). Some suggest that the uniqueness of negative information makes it more memorable (Kanouse and Hanson 1972; Lau 182, 2985; McGraw and Steenbergen

1997; Richey, et al 1982), while others believe that the increased attention given to negative information when first encountered accounts for our ability to recall it later (Kahn and Kenney 2000). Further, there is a growing consensus that emotion plays an important role in recall, with information soliciting a negative emotional reaction being more readily recalled than those associated with a neutral emotional response (Civettini and Redlawsk 2009: 128; Kensinger 2007). Given the public's expressed dislike for negative campaign information, it would not be a stretch to imagine a negative emotional response to it. Consequently, negative information about VP candidates would likely be more readily recalled. Whatever the reason, there is little doubt that "citizens are more likely to remember information if it is presented in a critical fashion." (Kahn and Kenney 2000: 84; see also Kahn and Kenney 2004: 67). Given these findings, we can expect voters to remember negative information presented to them by the media for longer than they will positive or neutral information and, thus, be more likely to use this information in the voting booth on election day.

A wealth of studies have documented just such an effect, showing that voters exposed to more negative information tend to learn more about the campaign and candidates. Studies suggest that "negative political advertising contains more information than positive political advertising" (Stevens 2005: 414), and many who argue that negative information increases turnout suggest this effect results from the knowledge voters gain from such information (Finkel and Geer 1998; Freedman and Goldstein 1999). Similarly, information gained from negative political advertising may increase campaign involvement and political engagement (Delli Carpini and Keeter, 1996; Goldstein and Freedman, 2002a). More directly, Lau, Sigelman, and Rovner (2007: 1183) surveyed a number of studies and concluded that negative information is "memorable and [generates] somewhat greater campaign-relevant knowledge." They point to studies showing a connection between negative information and knowledge of ballot measures (Arceneaux and Nickerson 2005), as well as knowledge about candidates (Niven 2006; Stevens 2005), including knowledge of a candidate's issue positions (Craig, Kane, and Gainous 2005; Niven 2006; Stevens 2005) and ideology (Iida 2005). Similarly, negative information has been linked to a number of other political behaviors, including turnout and vote choice, and attitudes such as candidate evaluations, campaign interest, and issue awareness (see Lau, Sigelman, and Rovner's 2007 for an overview of these studies). In fact, exposure to negative information has even been linked to higher levels of faith in elections (Geer 2006) and satisfaction with democracy (Stevens 2009).

At the same time, a number of studies they reviewed suggest no, or even detrimental, effects of negative information. Some have suggested that negative information exhibits such mixed effects because negative information influences some voters in different ways than others. For instance, Stevens (2005) points out that negative information likely leads more sophisticated voters to be more informed, but does not do the same for the less sophisticated. So even when negative information does not influence all voters, it will influence at least some portion of the electorate.

Given the heightened attention voters pay to negative information, their ability to better recall such information, and the wide ranging effects that negative information exhibits, it is likely that when the media coverage of VP candidates takes a negative tone these candidates will exert a stronger impact on vote choice. More negative media coverage will lead voters to learn more about VP candidates and hold the information they learn about them in memory long enough for it to influence their vote choice. Consequently, voters are more likely to form and consider their impressions of negatively portrayed VP candidates than they are to remember those who are portrayed more positively. To investigate this possibility, I consider the relationship between the VP impact measure utilized in the previous chapter and media negativity.

Measuring Media Negativity toward Vice Presidential Candidates

As Cohen (2008) notes, attempts to study the negativity of news coverage face several conceptual challenges. First, a negative story for one person may be a positive one for another. A single news report, for example, might portray one candidate negatively and another positively. It is, therefore, important to keep in mind the target of negativity when analyzing media content. Second, the source of negativity presents a particular challenge. Negative news can result from coverage of negative events (e.g., bad economic news or unsuccessful military campaigns) or from media interpretation of events (e.g., producing negative news even when no negative event exists). For many researchers this distinction is unimportant. Concerned more about the overall level of negativity in the news than about its source, they employ measures that capture the degree of negativity, no matter its source (Cohen 2008; Ragsdale 1997).

Here, however, I am more concerned about the degree to which voters come to know VP candidates. Linking a candidate to stories about negative events can certainly make an impression, likely a negative one, on voters, so the overall news negativity remains important here. At the same time, however, the media might present a story about a negative event, but portray a particular candidate in a more favorable light. This, too, is likely to shape voter perception of the candidate. Despite the negative tone of the story, the impression of the candidate it leaves on voters is likely to be more favorable. To address these two issues, I utilize two different measures of media negativity. First, I assess the overall tone of articles referencing candidates in presidential elections to see whether the media generally took a negative, neutral, or positive tone in stories concerning the candidate. This measure captures negativity that might result from coverage of bad events, as well as news that might convey a negative tone, even if no negative event occurred. Second, I gauge candidates' media images as unsatisfactory, neutral, or satisfactory. This measure ignores the overall tone of news referencing the candidates and focuses on the image of the candidate portrayed in these stories. Though these two variables seem quite similar, and are correlated strongly, they are not identical and appear to capture different underlying concepts.[1]

A story that takes on overall negative tone but portrays the candidate in a positive light would result in a low tone score and a high image score. For example, a September 17, 2004, story referencing Democratic VP candidate John Edwards negatively discusses the Kerry-Edwards campaign's failure to aggressively draw distinctions between their ticket's positions and those of their opponents, but notes that Edwards' inability to do so results from his "natural good-guy temperament." While the story takes on an overall negative tone (the failure of the campaign to operate effectively), the candidate himself receives positive coverage (Edwards is a good guy). Less than 1% of the stories analyzed here took a negative tone while positively portraying the candidate or vice versa. More commonly, news coverage took a neutral tone yet left the reader with a negative impression of the candidate, as was the case in an October 25, 1984, article referencing VP candidate Geraldine Ferraro. Even though the story was an even-handed treatment of allegations that a wealthy Chinatown merchant who donated to Ferraro's 1982 House campaign might be involved in organized crime, the story leaves readers with the impression that Ferraro may be connected to the mafia (an allegation that was frequently targeted at her husband during the Presidential race). Fully 9% of all the stories referencing VP candidates analyzed fell into this pattern.

So while the overall tone and candidate image variable are highly likely to produce the same score, this may not always be the case. Still, given the high degree of similarity between the two measures, I expect them to perform in the same way. More negative overall tone and more negative candidate image are expected to boost the impact that VP candidates have on Independent voters.

Capturing Overall Media Tone

To assess the overall tone of candidate media coverage, I again rely on the random sample of articles written about presidential campaign candidates (see Appendix B for details on sampling and coding procedures). Each of the selected stories about VP candidates was coded to indicate the overall tone of the story referencing the candidate. Stories offering a "negative" tone (whether due to coverage of a negative event or not) were scored a 1, those offering a "neutral" tone were scored a 2, and those with a "positive" tone were scored a 3. Each candidate's mean overall media tone score was then calculated. Table 4.1 presents the overall mean media tone scores for each presidential and VP candidate since 1970.

Table 4.1: Overall Tone of Media Coverage of Presidential and Vice Presidential Candidates, 1972-2008

	1972	1976	1980	1984	1988	1992	1996	2000	2004	2008
Democratic Presidential Candidate	1.92	1.83	1.76	1.90	1.90	2.00	1.88	1.86	2.00	2.11
Republican Presidential Candidate	1.78	1.92	1.85	1.80	1.80	1.76	1.72	1.73	1.58	1.71
Democratic Vice Presidential Candidate	2.10	2.00	1.92	2.00	2.08	2.15	2.13	1.74	2.00	2.14
Republican Vice Presidential Candidate	2.13	2.00	2.00	1.85	1.89	1.68	1.90	1.81	1.73	1.74

Notes: Cell entries are overall media tone scores, calculated as the overall tone of stories referencing the candidate. Overall tone measured as: 1 = "negative"; 2= "neutral"; 3 = "positive." See Appendix B for details on coding.

As this table illustrates, the media takes a generally neutral tone in stories referencing candidates in presidential elections. On the whole, presidential and VP candidates averaged a tone score of about 1.90, or about "neutral," on the three point scale. And the media appears to treat the bottom of the ticket more favorably than the top: while presidential candidates averaged a media tone score of 1.84, VP candidates averaged 1.95.[2] At the same time, Democratic candidates appear to draw slightly more positive mentions than their Republican counterparts. While Republican presidential and VP candidates average about 1.77 and 1.87, respectively, Democratic candidates rated 1.92 and 2.03.[3]

While the media generally treated candidates in a neutral manner, they targeted some with much more negativity than others. While Barack Obama, in the 2008 campaign, exhibited the highest overall tone score of all presidents (2.11), the preceding presidential race saw George W. Bush rate the lowest (1.58) of all presidents since the 1970s. Similarly, Dan Quayle holds the distinction of being the VP candidate with the most negative overall tone rating of 1.68, while Al Gore (in 1992) and Joe Biden (2008) rate the highest at 2.15 and 2.14, respectively.

Measuring Candidate Media Image

To capture the media's portrayal of candidate image, I coded each of the selected stories about VP candidates to indicate how satisfied a (hypothetical) campaign manager would be with their "candidate's image/description" in the story. Stories with which a campaign manager would likely be "unsatisfied" were scored a 1 and those with which he/she would be "satisfied" were scored a 3, while those with which the campaign manager was likely to be "neither satisfied nor dissatisfied" were scored a 2. Each candidate's mean overall image score was then calculated. Table 4.2 presents the overall candidate image scores for each presidential and VP candidate since 1970.

Table 4.2: Presidential and Vice Presidential Candidate Image, 1972-2008

	1972	1976	1980	1984	1988	1992	1996	2000	2004	2008
Democratic Presidential Candidate	1.76	1.76	1.54	1.75	1.76	1.84	1.77	1.55	1.99	2.18
Republican Presidential Candidate	1.63	1.65	1.67	1.65	1.65	1.36	1.54	1.61	1.48	1.73
Democratic Vice Presidential Candidate	2.20	2.09	2.14	2.00	2.35	2.29	2.04	1.93	2.07	2.12
Republican Vice Presidential Candidate	1.73	1.75	2.07	1.75	1.55	1.42	1.83	1.56	1.30	1.63

Notes: Cell entries are candidate media image scores, calculated as the overall candidate image portrayed in stories referencing the candidate. Candidate image measured as: 1 = "unsatisfactory"; 2= "neither satisfactory nor unsatisfactory"; 3 = "satisfactory." See Appendix B for details on coding.

As this table illustrates, candidates typically garner a neutral media image. On the whole, presidential and VP candidates averaged a media image score of about 1.79, or about "neutral," on the three point scale.

At the same time, VP media images appear to be slightly more positive than those of their running mates. While VP candidates averaged a media image score of 1.89, presidential candidates only averaged 1.69.[4] Similarly, Democratic candidates exhibit more positive media images than Republicans. While Republican presidential and VP candidates average about 1.60 and 1.66, respectively, Democratic candidates rated 1.79 and 2.12.[5]

Even though the media generally portrays candidates in a neutral manner, some candidates had much more positive images than others. While Barack Obama had the most positive media image score of all presidents (2.18) in the 2008 campaign, George H.W. Bush suffered from the worst media image (scoring just 1.36 on the three point scale) in his 1992 campaign. Similarly, Dick Cheney's media image (a score of 1.30) in the 2004 campaign was the worst of all VP candidates since 1970, while Lloyd Bentsen's image was the best, with a score of 2.35.

Media Negativity and Vice Presidential Candidate Impact

So it appears that while the media tend to cover VP candidates less negatively than their presidential running mates, there are still some VPs who receive much more negative coverage than others. Could this be the reason that some VP candidates affect voters more than others? Despite expectations, the evidence suggests not. Figure 4.1 illustrates the connection between the negativity of media coverage received by VP candidates and their impact on Independent voters. Somewhat surprisingly, the data suggest that media negativity plays virtually no role in predicting which VP candidates will affect voters most.[6]

While media negativity does not appear to predict the overall percentage of Independent voters affected, it is possible that negative coverage of a VP candidate might lead to lower support for his/her ticket, in particular. To investigate the directional hypothesis that negative coverage of VP candidates drives voters away from their tickets, I correlated the raw "percent of Independent voters affected" with the overall tone measure.[7] For both Democratic and Republican VP candidates, the correlations prove to be statistically insignificant and substantively very small, though they are in the expected direction. For Democratic VP candidates, more positive media coverage is associated with slightly more support for the Democratic ticket, whereas more positive media coverage of Republican VP candidates is associated with

Figure 4.1: Overall Media Tone and Vice Presidential Impact on Independent Voters, 1972-2008

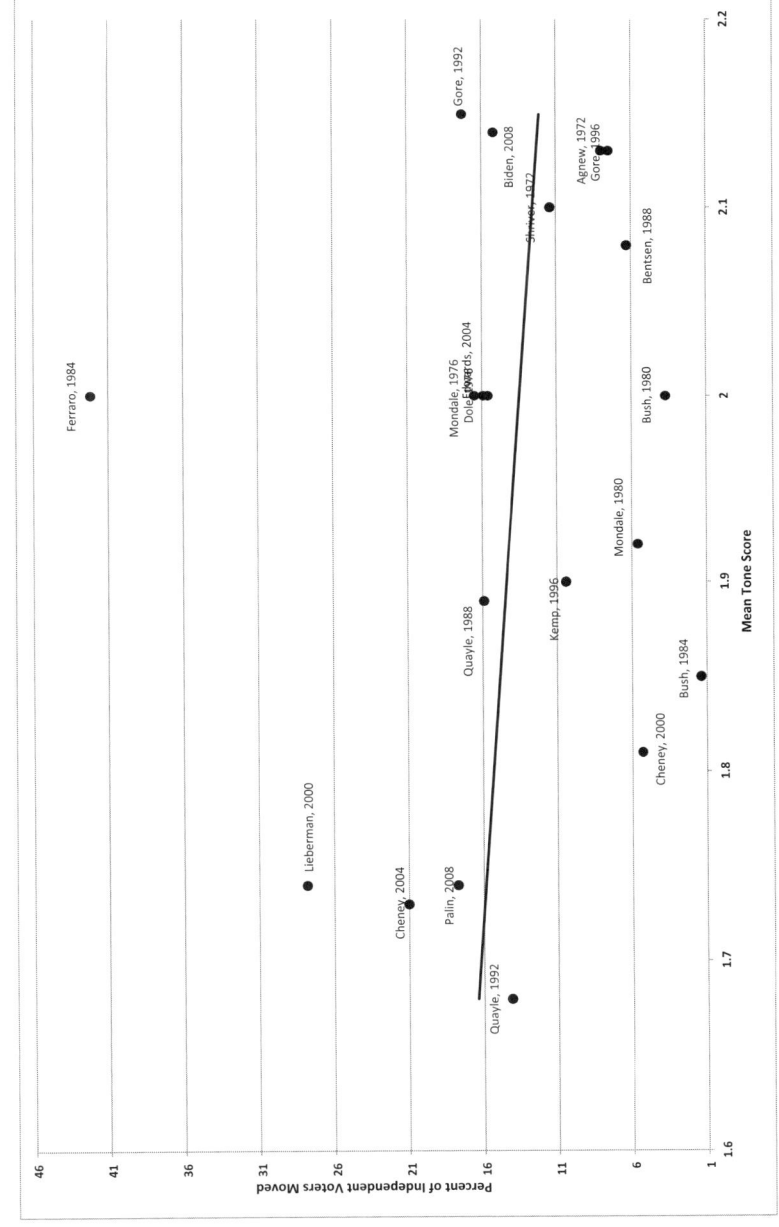

Note: Overall media tone scores range from 1 to 3 (see Appendix B for details on coding), Percent of Independent voters affected is the absolute value of the measure reported in Figure 2.1. The bivariate correlation for this relationship is -0.125 (p=0.601, two-tailed).

marginally less support for the Democratic ticket (and thus, more support for the Republican ticket).[8]

Much the same results arise with regard to candidates' media images. As Figure 4.2 illustrates, the relationship between the negativity of a candidate's media image and the impact that candidate exerts on voters at election time fails to emerge.[9] Contradicting the common belief that media negativity greatly affects voters, the data does not show that candidates with more negative media images affect voter decision making more.

I again investigated the directional hypothesis that negative media images of VP candidates drive voters away from their tickets by correlating the raw "percent of Independent voters affected" with the overall tone measure. Similar to the media negativity findings, the correlations for VP candidates of both parties are statistically insignificant and substantively very small, though they are in the expected direction. For Democratic VP candidates, more positive media images are associated with more support for the Democratic ticket, whereas more positive media images of Republican VP candidates are associated with less support for the Democratic ticket (and thus, more support for the Republican ticket).[10]

Despite a plethora of studies suggesting that negative media coverage greatly impacts voter decision making, the results here suggest that when it comes to VP candidates, the negativity of media coverage does not cause voters to pay attention to their feelings about these candidates when casting a ballot.[11] Perhaps media negativity plays such an inconsequential role because of the generally neutral tone of coverage received by VP candidates during campaigns. The remarkably neutral tone with which the media covers VP candidates during the presidential campaign season most likely leaves voters with neither a positive nor a negative sense of the candidate. As a result, voters tend to consider their feelings about candidates they hear more about, no matter the tone of the coverage (as we saw in the previous chapter).

Media Negativity and Incumbent Candidates

While not all VP candidates draw a large volume of negative media coverage, there is one subset of these candidates who are more likely to be more consistently covered, possibly in a negative manner. Incumbent VP candidates stand in the media spotlight not only during the election season but also for the three years between elections. Since the media exposes voters to incumbent candidates more often and more consistently than non-incumbent candidates, voters will probably come

Figure 4.2: Candidate Image and Vice Presidential Impact on Independent Voters, 1972-2008

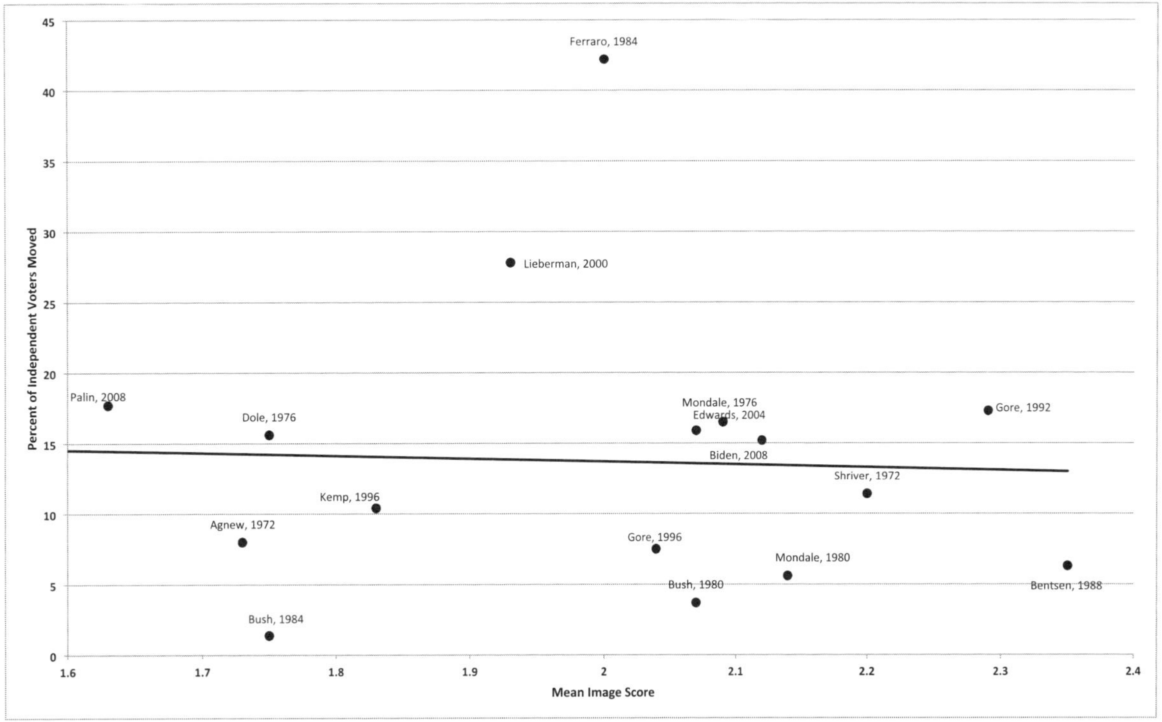

Note: Image scores range from 1 to 3 (see Appendix B for details on coding). Percent of Independent voters affected is the absolute value of the measure reported in Figure 2.1. The bivariate correlation for this relationship is -0.065 (p=0.786, two-tailed).

to know incumbent VP candidates better than non-incumbent VP candidates. Consequently, it seems likely that incumbent candidates who are covered more negatively during their first terms will exhibit a greater impact on voters at the time of reelection.

To assess whether voters are more affected by incumbent VP candidates who are more negatively covered during their first terms more than those who attract more positive coverage, I compare the media negativity given to incumbent VPs during their first terms to the impact they had on voters at reelection time. During the time period studied here, five VP candidates ran as incumbents standing for reelection to that position: Mondale in 1980, Bush in 1984, Quayle in 1992, Gore in 1996, and Cheney in 2004. Using the same coding schemes for overall media tone and candidate image described above, a sample of stories about these incumbent VP candidates during their first term in office was coded as having either a negative, neutral, or positive tone, and each candidate's image was coded as either unsatisfactory, satisfactory, or neither.[12] Each candidate's mean media tone score for the non-campaign season was then calculated.

These mean overall tone scores, along with each incumbent's voter impact, are reported on Table 4.3. As expected, incumbent VP candidates receiving more negative media coverage exhibit a greater impact on voters. Dick Cheney, the incumbent who had the greatest impact on voters, received the most negative media coverage during his first term in office of any incumbent VP. From questioning the accounting practices of Halliburton Corporation during his tenure as chief executive (Berenson and Bergman 2002) to scrutinizing his participation in a pheasant hunt some called a "mass killing" (Bumiller 2003), the media did not hesitate to negatively report on Cheney. More than 37% of the media coverage received by Cheney during his first term was negative while less than 3% was positive, leading to his mean overall tone score of just 1.65.

On the other end of the scale, Walter Mondale received entirely neutral coverage resulting in a solidly neutral overall media tone score. About the worst thing said about him was that, though he "was by general agreement the most decent and certainly one of the most liberal leaders of the Democratic party," he was involved in a "political blitz" attacking Ted Kennedy in order to keep him "out of play" in the 1980 Presidential election (Reston 1979). Not surprisingly Mondale exhibits the weakest impact on voters of all incumbent VP candidates. Uniformly, the candidates affecting voters more were the candidates receiving lower mean tone scores and higher percentages of negative coverage.[13]

**Table 4.3: Overall Tone of Non-Election Year Media Coverage
and Impact of Incumbent Vice Presidential Candidates
on Independent Voters, 1972-2008**

Candidate	% of Independents Affected	Mean Tone of Coverage	% of Coverage that is Negative	% of Coverage that is Neutral	% of Coverage that is Positive
Cheney (2004)	21.0	1.7	37.8	59.5	2.7
Quayle (1992)	14.1	1.8	28.2	66.7	5.1
Gore (1996)	7.5	1.9	20.0	73.3	6.7
Mondale (1980)	5.6	2.0	0.0	100.0	0.0
Bush (1984)	3.7	1.9	12.2	87.8	0.0

Note: Mean tone of coverage scores range from 1 to 3 (see Appendix B for details on coding), Percent of Independent voters affected is the absolute value of the measure reported in Figure 2.1. The bivariate correlation for the relationship between mean tone of coverage and voters affected is -0.909 (p=0.032, two-tailed) and the correlation for the relationship between percent of coverage that is negative and voters affected is 0.888 (p=0.044, two-tailed).

Much the same result emerges with regard to incumbent VP candidates' media images. Table 4.4 reports the mean candidate image score for each incumbent candidate, along with each candidate's voter impact. As expected, incumbent candidates who had lower media images tend to exhibit the largest impact on voters.[14] Once again, Dick Cheney, who influenced the votes of more than 20% of Independent voters, ranks lowest among all incumbent VP candidates when it comes to media image. Cheney was accused of "not being a good sport" (Bumiller 2003), of exaggerating the truth about links between Al Qaeda and Iraq (Schmitt 2003), of sounding like "someone who has something to hide" (Dean 2002) regarding the White House energy task force he headed, and of trying to shift payment of his residential electric bill to the U.S. Navy (Shenon 2001). With nearly 65% of the stories about him portraying a negative image and less than one percent of them offering a positive image, Cheney's resulting media image score of 1.36 is far below average. Conversely, Walter Mondale who was said to possess "an intellect as stunning as the president's, but more compassionate" (Tolchin 1978) and Al Gore who displayed an "earnest, Boy Scout manner" (Berke 1994) rated much higher than Cheney with image scores of 1.92, but affect the votes of less than 10% of Independent voters each.

Table 4.4: Candidate Image in Non-Election Year Media Coverage and Vice Presidential Impact on Independent Voters, 1972-2008

Candidate	% of Independents Affected	Mean Candidate Image	% of Coverage that is Unsatisfactory	% of Coverage that is Neutral	% of Coverage that is Satisfactory
Cheney (2004)	21.0	1.4	64.9	34.4	0.6
Quayle (1992)	14.1	1.5	53.1	44.4	2.5
Gore (1996)	7.5	1.9	34.3	60.0	5.7
Mondale (1980)	5.6	1.9	10.5	86.8	2.6
Bush (1984)	3.7	1.8	19.3	78.3	2.4

Note: Mean candidate image scores range from 1 to 3 (see Appendix B for details on coding), Percent of Independent voters affected is the absolute value of the measure reported in Figure 2.1. The bivariate correlation for the relationship between mean candidate image and voters affected is -0.934 (p=0.020, two-tailed) and the correlation for the relationship between percent of coverage that is unsatisfactory and voters affected is 0.943 (p=0.016, two-tailed).

So it appears that, in general, negative media coverage does not lead voters to consider their feelings about VP candidates more at election time. Importantly, however, at reelection time, voters do consider their feelings about incumbent vice presidential candidates who have been covered more negatively in the previous three years when casting a ballot.

Summary

This chapter focused on the role that media negativity plays in making voters consider their feelings about some vice presidential candidates more than others. The analyses compared the overall tone of media coverage of VP candidates, as well as the candidates' images in the media, to the impact they had on voters. The chapter's findings revealed that while media negativity toward VP candidates does not appear to increase the impact that these candidates generally have on voters, negative media coverage is important for incumbent VP candidates. Voters are swayed by their feelings about incumbent candidates who are covered more negatively during their first term in office more than they are swayed by candidates who receive more positive coverage.

The next chapter moves beyond general assessments of media content to explore whether the media's focus on certain candidate characteristics affects the impact that these candidates have on voters.

After reviewing reasons why voters are likely to pay more attention to the information about key sociodemographic characteristics of candidates in presidential elections, I test to see if media coverage of such vice presidential candidate characteristics helps to explain why some VP candidates matter more to voters than others.

Notes

[1] The mean overall tone and candidate image scores for VP candidates correlate at 0.599 (sig. at 0.000), and 85.8% of stories analyzed exhibit agreement on the overall tone score and candidate image score (i.e., both are negative, both are neutral, or both are positive).

[2] This difference is statistically significant at p = 0.016, two-tailed.

[3] The difference in scores between parties is statistical significant for both presidential (p=0.002, two-tailed) and VP candidates (p=0.020, two tailed).

[4] This difference is statistically significant at p = 0.015 two-tailed.

[5] The difference in scores between parties is statistical significant for both presidential (p=0.012, two-tailed) and VP candidates (p=0.000, two tailed).

[6] The bivariate correlation for this relationship is -0.125 (p=0.601, two-tailed). Not surpsingly, this insignificant results remains when the control variables for economic conditions and presidential popularity are included in a multivariate model.

[7] Positive values of the raw percentage of Independent voters moved measure indicate a more favorable chance of voting for the Democratic ticket (and lower chance of voting for the Republican ticket), while negative values indicate the opposite (lower probability of voting for the Democratic ticket and higher probability of voting for the Republican ticket).

[8] The correlation for Democratic VP candidates is 0.046 (p=0.327) and the correlation for the Republican VP candidates is -0.004 (p=0.248).

[9] The bivariate correlation for this relationship is -0.065 (p=0.786, two-tailed). This insignificant results remains in a multivariate model that includes controls for economic conditions and presidential popularity.

[10] The correlation for Democratic VP candidates is 0.082 (p=0.277) and the correlation for the Republican VP candidates is -0.030 (p=0.352).

[11] Not surprisingly, these relationships fail to emerge when subjected to controls for the economic conditions at the time of the election and popularity of the sitting president. When the economic and presidential popularity control variable included on Table 3.3 are included along with the media negativity variables presented here, the relationships between overall tone of media coverage and candidate image remain insignificant.

[12] The same search and sampling strategy described in Appendix B was used to code 25% of all stories referencing any incumbent VP candidate during the period of time between inauguration day of the first term in office and the beginning of the reelection campaign season (Labor Day of the reelection year).

[13] The bivariate correlation for the relationship between mean tone of coverage and absolute value of voters affected is -0.909 (p=0.032, two-tailed) and the correlation for the relationship between percent of coverage that is

negative and absolute value of voters affected is 0.888 (p=0.044, two-tailed). The very small sample of incumbent VPis prevents a test of the directional hypothesis that negative coverage of a party's incumbent VP leads to less support for his ticket. Such an analysis requires splitting the sample along partisan lines, and the resulting sub-sample sizes are too small to run meaningful statistical analyses.

[14] The bivariate correlation for the relationship between mean candidate image and voters moved is -0.934 (p=0.020, two-tailed) and the correlation for the relationship between percent of coverage that is unsatisfactory and voters moved is 0.943 (p=0.016, two-tailed).

5

How Media Coverage of
Sociodemogaphics Matters

The analyses presented in the previous chapter suggests that the content of media coverage can affect how much impact vice presidential candidates have on voters. When incumbent candidates receive sustained negative media coverage, voters are more likely to let their feelings about the candidates influence their vote choices. This chapter further examines the content of media coverage, focusing on coverage of candidates' sociodemographic characteristics. The vote decision can be a cumbersome one involving sifting through volumes of information about the candidates, their parties, the policy stances, and many other factors. Since most voters do not have the time (and perhaps ability) to devote to gathering and assessing all available information, they often employ information shortcuts. For voters seeking a quick and easy source of information, candidate characteristics serve as readily available indicators of important information about the candidates' likely ideology and policy stances, as well as their ability to fulfill the duties of office.

This chapter investigates whether shining a light on the sociodemograhic characteristics of vice presidential candidates matters. It will investigate whether vice presidential candidates receiving more media coverage, particularly more negative coverage, of key sociodemographic characteristics will impact voter decision making more than those who receive less (and less negative) coverage. After reviewing the reasons why such candidate characteristics are likely to influence voters, I construct measures capturing media coverage of these characteristics and illustrate how some VP candidates receive more coverage of this sort than others. I then explore the relationship between such media coverage and VP impact on voters, finding that coverage of some characteristics matters more than others. While media mentions of candidates' race and marital status play little role in explaining VP impact on voters, media coverage of candidates' sex and religious preference helps explain why some VP candidates are far more meaningful to voters than others.

Candidate Characteristics as Information Shortcuts

Presidential campaigns offer voters innumerable bits of information aimed at helping them make their vote choices. Scholars have long argued that voters find it unreasonably costly to use all the information available to them and thus seek to exploit low cost information that contains relevant details about the candidates (Downs 1957). The use of such readily available information offers voters a way to "tame the tide" (Graber 1984) of campaign information washing over them. Operating as "cognitive misers" who employ a form of low information rationality (Fiske and Taylor 1991; Lau and Sears 1986; Popkin 1991; Simon 1957, 1985), voters employ information shortcuts (or cognitive heuristics) to efficiently arrive at an informed vote choice (Kahneman, Slovic, and Tversky 1982; Nisbett and Ross 1980; Popkin 1991). Frequently these heuristics will take the form of stereotypes or generalizations about groups and their members (Fiske and Taylor 1991; McDermott 1998; Ottati and Wyer 1990; Rahn 1993; Riggle, et al. 1992). For instance, voters might rely on information about candidate characteristics such as race, gender, religious preference, and marital status to provide important clues about a candidate's likely ideology, policy stances, or performance in office. In fact, candidate characteristics have been argued to be "possibly the most important (or at least most frequently employed)" heuristic used by voters (Lau and Redlawsk 2001: 954), and voters have a long history of relying on candidate characteristics, particularly race and gender, when casting a vote.

When it comes to assessing candidates based on certain characteristics, key stereotypes appear to come into play. Voters tend to view African-American candidates as more liberal (McDermott 2009; Sigelman, et al 1995; Williams 1990), more willing to help the poor (Williams 1990), more sympathetic to disadvantaged groups (Sigelman, et al 1995), and more likely to care about racial issues (McDermott 2009) than other candidates. Voters also tend to "use candidate gender as a "low-information shortcut" to estimate the candidate's policy stands," and ideology, which subsequently affects vote choice (Sabonmatsu 2002: 21; see also Dolan 1998; Fox and Smith 1998; Kahn 1996; McDermott 1997; McDermott 1998; Paolino 1995). Voters tend to see female candidates as better able to handle compassion and women's rights issues, and to view them as more liberal, Democratic, and feminist (Huddy and Terkildsen 1993; Leeper 1991; Kahn 1994; Matland 1994; Rosenwasser and Seale 1988; Sanbomatsu 2002; Sapiro 1981-82). They also believe female candidates to be more honest, sophisticated, attractive, aggressive, strong, and active (Kaid, et al. 1984; Leeper 1991; Sapiro 1981-82), though they also tend to rate them lower (Fox and Smith 1998) and believe that candidates with stereotypically masculine traits are better suited to holding public office (Huddy and Terkildsen 1993; Rosenwasser and Dean 1989). Importantly, these race and gender related perceptions play a role in voter decision making (McDermott 2009).

Though less extensive, there is also evidence that voters are likely to employ candidates' religious preference and marital status as cognitive shortcuts as well. McDermott (2009) illustrates that voter stereotyping of evangelical candidates as more conservative, trustworthy, and competent affects their vote choice, and Berinsky and Mendelberg (2005) find that campaigns can cue stereotypes that lead Jewish candidates to lose support. Similarly, almost one-third of voters report caring about a candidate's marital status (CBS News 2011) and some political pundits argue that marital status remains hugely important to voters and that "Americans seem to feel better about a candidate when they see the de rigueur image of a husband and wife smiling and waving together" (Cherlin 2011).

In addition to using candidate characteristics as shortcuts to their performance in office, voters may also believe that candidates with whom they share characteristics will personally benefit them more. Research shows that people tend to see candidates sharing characteristics with them as also sharing their values and concerns (Gay 2001). Further, voters tend to believe that political elites who share characteristics with them will be more responsive to their needs (Gilliam 1996; Tate 1993, 2001; Bobo and Gilliam 1990; Gurin, Hatchett, and Jackson 1989; Pantoja and Segura 2003). Voters might also take common characteristics to mean that they will have more access to the candidate and an "assurance that two-way communication is possible" (Fenno 1978).

Whatever information voters garner from candidate characteristics, there is little doubt that they must be aware of these characteristics in order for them to affect their vote choice. Consequently, I expect that when the media more frequently discusses candidates' characteristics, voters will come to weigh their feelings about the candidates more heavily. Given the public's tendency to pay more attention to negative information, it is likely that candidates receiving the most negative coverage of their traits will exhibit the greatest impact on voters.

Measuring Media Coverage of Candidate Characteristics

Using the random sample of articles written about presidential campaign candidates (see Appendix B for details on sampling and coding procedures), I measure the volume and tone of articles written about four candidate characteristics – race/ethnicity, sex, religious preference, and marital status. Each of the selected stories about vice presidential candidates was first coded to indicate which, if any, of the characteristics and traits were mentioned. Any reference to a candidate's race/ethnicity, sex, religious preference, or marital status was noted, regardless of the context within which it was mentioned. Then each story that mentioned a characteristic was scored to indicate whether the coverage of that characteristic/trait was negative (coded 1), neutral/balanced (coded 2), or positive (coded 3). The context within which and the tone with which the characteristic was discussed were considered when making this coding decision.

Taking the characteristic of candidate sex as an example, when VP candidate Geraldine Ferraro's gender is referenced in the context of her nomination being nothing more than Mondale's way of "getting the women's vote," (Gargan 1984) this is considered a negative treatment of her gender. In contrast, when Sarah Palin's nomination is referred to as a "healthy development" because it challenges the tradition of an all-male Presidential race, the mention receives a positive rating (Kinsley 2008). And neutral ratings went to stories like those that referred to Ferraro wanting to be "the first women to be elected vice president" (Perlez 1984a) or Palin as only the second woman to participate in a VP debate (Seelye 2008). Coding decisions were made similarly for the other characteristics.

Volume of Media Coverage of Candidate Characteristics

Table 5.1 summarizes the overall volume of media coverage of presidential and VP characteristics and traits. Given the candidacy of Barack Obama, it is perhaps no surprise that the media has focused more on race/ethnicity when it comes to presidential candidates than to vice presidential ones. While 10.2% of the media coverage of Barack Obama mentioned his race, only Geraldine Ferraro's Italian heritage drew a single press mention.[1] In contrast, the media seem much more likely to mention VP candidates' sex, religious preference, and marital status.

Table 5.1: Volume of Media Coverage of Candidate Characteristics

	Vice Presidential Candidates			Presidential Candidates		
	Minimum	Maximum	Mean (Std. Dev.)	Minimum	Maximum	Mean (Std. Dev.)
Race	0	0.8	0.04 (0.18)	0	10.2	0.60 (2.28)
Sex	0	28.5	2.23 (6.82)	0	0.8	0.07 (0.19)
Religious Preference	0	15.4	2.25 (4.53)	0	4.8	1.47 (1.56)
Marital Status	0	12.4	4.25 (3.74)	0	4.6	1.91 (1.24)

Note: Cell entries are percent of all media coverage mentioning candidate that discuss the characteristic.

[handwritten: does gender matter even more now? not having gender balance seen as bad.]

Since all presidential candidates have been men, it is no wonder that, on average, less than one-tenth of one percent (0.07%) of presidential media coverage mentions the sex of the candidate. Given the VP candidacies of Sarah Palin and Geraldine Ferraro, we would expect the media to mention sex more when it comes to the bottom of the ticket, and the data bear out this expectation. On average, more than 2% of all media coverage of VP candidates since 1970 mentions candidates' sex. Not surprisingly, Ferraro, as the first female VP candidate in American history, garnered the most media attention to her sex with more than 28% of the media coverage of her mentioning the fact that she was a woman. More than two decades later, the media were far less fixated on Palin's gender, mentioning it in only 12.9% of their coverage of her.

Similarly, VP candidates Geraldine Ferraro and Joe Lieberman drew more than the average amount of media attention to their religious preferences. While slightly more than 15% of the coverage of Ferraro mentioned her Catholic faith, a little more than 14% mentioned Lieberman's Jewish heritage. No other candidate, presidential or vice presidential, attracted nearly as much attention to their faith, with only 1.2% of the coverage of all other VP candidates mentioning their religious preferences. *[handwritten: → true in future for Romney + Biden.]*

The media were more even-handed in their coverage of candidates' marital statuses, though VP candidates still garnered more attention in this regard than their running mates. While less than 2% of the media coverage of presidential candidates mentioned marital status, more than 4% of VP coverage did so. The 2008 election saw the media the most preoccupied with VP candidates' marriages, with 12.4% of Palin's coverage and 10% of Biden's coverage mentioning their marital statuses. The next five candidates whose marriages were most scrutinized by the media were also VP candidates (Gore, 1996; Edwards, 2004; Cheney, 2000; Ferraro, 1984; Quayle, 1992).[2]

[handwritten: ironic given the first family image]

Negativity of Media Coverage of Candidate Characteristics

Table 5.2 summarizes media negativity surrounding candidate characteristics by reporting (a) the percent of all stories mentioning presidential and vice presidential candidates that negatively discuss each characteristic and (b) the percent of stories about each characteristic taking a negative tone.[3] As this table suggests, the media rarely go negative with regard to candidate characteristics. On average, candidates' race/ethnicity, sex, religion, and marital status are discussed in a negative manner in less than one percent of the total coverage of candidates. In fact, the media never negatively report on VP candidates' race/ethnicity and at worst negatively discuss candidates' marital statuses in about one-fifth of one percent of stories about VP candidates. Focusing only on stories that mention candidate characteristics reveals much the same picture, with slightly more than 2% of all media coverage of VP marital status taking a negative tone and less than one percent of coverage of VP sex and religious preference garnering negative attention.

Table 5.2: Negativity of Media Coverage of Vice Presidential Candidate Characteristics

	Percent of All Coverage that Negatively Mentions Characteristic			Percent of Mentions of Characteristic that are Negative		
	Minimum	Maximum	Mean (Std. Dev.)	Minimum	Maximum	Mean (Std. Dev.)
Race	0	0	0.00 (0.00)	0	0	0.00 (0.00)
Sex	0	0.8	0.04 (0.18)	0	2.7	0.14 (0.60)
Religious Preference	0	0.8	0.04 (0.18)	0	5	0.25 (1.12)
Marital Status	0	2.4	0.22 (0.62)	0	25	2.29 (6.55)

While little evidence of overwhelming media negativity toward VP candidates emerges, some VP candidates suffer a much larger share of negativity than others. As we saw above, only Geraldine Ferraro and Sarah Palin attracted media coverage of their gender, and examination of media negativity reveals that only Ferraro received negative coverage in this regard. While none of the coverage discussing Palin's sex was negative, nearly 3% of the coverage discussing Ferraro's sex painted her gender in an unfavorable light. Similarly, while only Ferraro and Lieberman drew mentions about their religious preferences, Lieberman suffered no media negativity in this regard while 5% of the media discussions of Ferraro's Catholic faith turned critical. While the marriages of many VP candidates became media fodder more than other characteristics, only three suffered negativity on this front. Again, the media negatively covered Geraldine Ferraro, along with Dan Quayle and Sarah Palin. Quayle attracted the most negativity, with one-quarter of the media stories about his wife's polarizing mentions of "family values" during campaign appearances. Almost 17% of stories focusing on Ferraro's marriage were negative, focusing primarily on her husband's business dealings and possible ties to organized crime. In contrast, only 4% of the media coverage criticized Palin's marriage, particularly her husband's role in possible ethical violations relating to the firing of an Alaska State Trooper.

Still despite this little negative now on gender → become more inclusive.

Media Coverage of Candidate Characteristics and Vice Presidential Impact

The data show that some vice presidential candidates draw much more (and more negative) coverage of their personal characteristics. Perhaps this is the reason that voters' feelings about some VP candidates affect their votes more than others. Table 5.3 presents the level and negativity of media coverage of the four candidate characteristics examined here, along with the percent of independent voters affected by VP candidates. As this table suggests, VP candidates who receive more (and more negative) media coverage of their sex, religious preference, and to a lesser degree, marital status seem to influence more voters than those candidates who receive less (and less negative) coverage of these characteristics.

Looking first to the relationship between coverage of candidate sex and voter impact, we see that, not surprisingly, the two female candidates drew all the gender-related media coverage. Almost 29% of the media's coverage of Geraldine Ferraro mentioned that she was a woman while about 13% of Palin's coverage did so. Not only did the press mention Ferraro's sex more often, they did so in a more negative manner. While none of Palin's sex-related coverage turned negative, almost 3% of Ferraro's turned negative. The media's mistreatment of Ferraro has become legendary. Described by media voices as "pushy" and "feisty," (Carlin and Winfrey 2009), there was also a tendency to question her ability to perform because of her sex. During a *Meet the Press* interview, for example, Ferraro was asked, "Do you think the Soviets might be tempted to try to take advantage of you simply because you are a woman?" (Jamieson 1995: 107). In contrast, the media treated the fact that Sarah Palin was a woman in a much more positive manner. While Ferraro's nomination was cast as a ploy by Walter Mondale to get the women's vote (Gargan 1984), Palin's nomination was heralded as a "watershed event" (Warner 2008) and she was lauded as a good role model for young women. Reports of her candidacy quoted sources saying it was "cool to have a young woman on the ticket" (Fairbanks 2008) and that it was "good to have a woman [in the Presidential race]" (Capuzzo 2008).

Table 5.3: Media Coverage of Vice Presidential Candidate Characteristics and Vice Presidential Impact on Independent Voters, 1972-2008

	% of Independents Affected	% of all Coverage Mentioning Characteristic	% of all Coverage that Negatively Mentions Characteristic	% of Mentions of Characteristic that are Negative
		Candidate Sex	*Candidate Sex*	*Candidate Sex*
Ferraro	42.2	28.5	0.8	2.7
Palin	17.7	12.9	0.0	0.0
All Others	12.2	0.0	0.0	0.0
		Candidate Religion	*Candidate Religion*	*Candidate Religion*
Ferraro	42.2	15.4	0.8	5.0
Lieberman	27.8	14.3	0.0	0.0
All Others	11.6	0.0	0.0	0.0
		Candidate Marital Status	*Candidate Marital Status*	*Candidate Marital Status*
Ferraro	42.2	9.2	1.5	16.7
Quayle (199:	14.1	9.5	2.4	25.0
Palin	17.7	12.4	0.5	4.0
Cheney (200	5.3	8.2	0.0	0.0
Biden	15.2	10.0	0.0	0.0
All Others	12.3	2.4	0.0	0.0
		Candidate Race/Ethnicity	*Candidate Race/Ethnicity*	*Candidate Race/Ethnicity*
Ferraro	42.2	0.8	0.0	0.0
All Others	12.5	0.0	0.0	0.0

Notes: For coverage of candidate sex: 2.3% of all coverage positively mentioned Ferraro's sex and 3.5% positively mentioned Palin's sex; 8.10% of the mentions of Ferraro's sex were positive and 26.9% of the mentions of Palin's sex were positive. For religion, 3.1% of all coverage positively mentioned Lieberman's religious preference, while 21.4% of the coverage of his religion was positive. None of the coverage of Ferraro's religions preference was positive. For marital status, 1.5% of all of the coverage of Palin's marital status was positive, and 12% of the coverage of her marital status was positive. For all other candidates reported, all coverage of marital status was neutral. All coverage of Ferraro's race was neutral.

While the media treated Ferraro and Palin very differently, the mere mention of their gender appears to be associated with the impact these candidates made on voters.[4] Ferraro, who received the most and the most negative coverage of her gender, was the most influential VP candidate of the past forty years. Palin, the only other candidate to receive any media coverage of her gender, was the fourth most influential candidate occupying the bottom of the ticket. Importantly, these relationships withstand the addition of control variables for economic conditions and presidential popularity.[5] As Table 5.4 illustrates, even after accounting for these factors, VP candidates who receive more (and more negative) coverage of their sex affect the votes of more Independent voters than those who receive less, and/or less negative, coverage.[6]

Table 5.4: Media Coverage of Candidate Sex and
Vice Presidential Impact, 1972-2008

	I.	II.	III.
Percent of All Coverage Mentioning Candidate Sex	0.937 ***	----	----
Percent of All Coverage Negatively Mentioning Candidate Sex	----	37.844 ***	----
Percent of Mentions of Candidate Sex that are Negative	----	----	11.213 ***
Presidential Approval	0.120	0.128	0.128
Economic Conditions	0.075	-0.296	-0.296
Constant	4.526	5.396	5.396
Number of Cases	20	20	20
Adjusted R-squared	0.402	0.523	0.434

Note: Cell entries are unstandardized OLS regression coefficients. Dependent variable is absolute value of "Percent of Independent Voters Affected" as reported in Figure 2.1.
***p<0.000 (two-tailed).

The results with regard to media coverage of VP religious preferences offer just as striking a picture. As Table 5.3 reveals, Ferraro's Catholic faith and Lieberman's Jewish heritage drew the media's attention to about the same degree. While about 15% of Ferraro's coverage mentioned her Catholicism, about 14% of the media's mentions of Lieberman discussed his Jewish faith. Once again, we see the media treating Ferraro more negatively. While none of Lieberman's religiously-related coverage was negative, about 5% of the time the media discussed Ferraro's faith, the stories, centered largely on her break with the Catholic Church on the issue of abortion, took on a negative tone. Ferraro's position that she "personally agree[d] with Roman Catholic doctrine, which opposes abortion without exception, but that she would not impose her views on others," (Perlez 1984a) drew criticism from leaders of the Catholic Church that were repeatedly played over in the media. While Archbishop O'Connor "accused Mrs. Ferraro of misstating Catholic teaching on abortion" (Oreskes 1984), "Bishop James C. Timlin of the Diocese of Scranton attacked the Democratic Vice-Presidential candidate's position on abortion, calling it "absurd" and "not a rational position" (Perlez 1984b). As stories about Ferraro's faith and how it would affect her performance in office played out in the media, Ferraro attempted to assure the public that like John Kennedy, "her Catholicism would not influence her public policies" (Perlez 1984a) and that "if her religion ever interfered with her performance of her duties, she would quit" (Raines 1984).

While coverage of Ferraro's Catholic faith struck a discordant chord, their treatment of Lieberman's Jewish heritage offered the public a more melodious tune. Lieberman, who was portrayed as providing a "kind of moral armor that the party has not enjoyed since Jimmy Carter's first campaign in 1976," was said to have "given ethical, even theological ballast to Mr. Gore's effort to succeed a president widely perceived as, shall we say, situationally religious" (Raines 2000). Unlike the confrontational and divisive coverage of Ferraro's faith, Lieberman's religious appeal was described as reaching across denominational lines to reach fundamentalist and evangelical Protestants as well as conservative Catholics (Raines 2000). As Pat Robertson, the Christian Coalition chairman and founder, noted "With Lieberman, there's going to be some defection on moral issues and [those in the Bush campaign] have to be aware of that" (Berke 2000). Overall, the public was left with the impression that Lieberman's "religion provide[d] a common ground for values . . . that few would find objectionable" (Perez-Pena 2000).

The volume and negativity of the media's focus on these two candidates' religion helps explain why they rank among the most influential VP candidates of the last 40 years.[7] Given the media's repeated, and negative, attention to Ferraro it is becoming apparent why she is the most impactful VP candidate since 1970. At the same time, the media's focus on Joe Lieberman's religious preference suggests an answer as to why he ranks as the second most influential running mate over the same period. Again, as Table 5.5. reveals, these relationships withstand the imposition of controls for economic conditions and presidential popularity. Candidates who received more (and more negative) coverage of their religious preferences tended to affect more Independent voters.[8]

The results for coverage of candidate marital status and race prove to be less telling. As Table 5.3 reveals, the media have focused on the marital status of many VP candidates, but some garner more attention than others. The media seems to have fixated most on the marriages of 2008 candidates Palin and Biden, followed by Quayle, Ferraro, and Cheney (in 2000). Only two of these candidates, Ferraro and Palin, rate as highly influential when it comes to affecting voters, and, as we have seen, other aspects of media coverage help to explain their influence. Overall, then, the association between the volume of media coverage of candidates' marriages and VP impact on voters appears to be weak at best.[9]

Table 5.5: Media Coverage of Candidate Religious Preference and Vice Presidential Impact, 1972-2008

	I.	II.	III.
Percent of All Coverage Mentioning Candidate Religion	1.571 ***	----	----
Percent of All Coverage Negatively Mentioning Candidate Religion	----	37.844 ***	----
Percent of Mentions of Candidate Religion that are Negative	----	----	6.055 ***
Presidential Approval	-0.046	0.128	0.128
Economic Conditions	0.501	-0.296	-0.296
Constant	12.100	5.396	5.396
Number of Cases	20	20	20
Adjusted R-squared	0.541	0.434	0.434

Note: Cell entries are unstandardized OLS regression coefficients. Dependent variable is absolute value of "Percent of Independent Voters Affected" as reported in Figure 2.1. ***p<0.000 (two-tailed).

[handwritten: fans on what issue they become known for Quayle -family values.]

Interestingly, though, some candidates' marriages were more negatively discussed than others. In particular, the marriages of Geraldine Ferraro, Dan Quayle, and Sarah Palin received negative media attention, with Quayle receiving the brunt of the negativity. Fully a quarter of the times the media mentioned his marriage, they did so in a disparaging way. The press were especially fixated on Marilyn Quayle's Republican National Convention "family values" speech, which some felt had an "accusatory edge" (Safire 1992) and left the impression that "some life choices were better than others" (Rosenthal 1992). Mrs. Quayle's speech was reported to have taken aim particularly at "women who do not center their lives inside the home" (Safire 1992), a charge that reignited the media's attention to Dan Quayle's speech from months earlier attacking fictional television character Murphy Brown for "mocking the importance of fathers, by bearing a child alone and calling it just another 'life style choice'" (Wines 1992). Feeling the brunt of the media's harsh treatment of Mrs. Quayle, some wondered out loud if she had become "an electoral liability" (Rohter 1992).

Ferraro similarly suffered negative media coverage of her husband, John Zacarro's, business dealings and possible involvement with organized crime. Stories questioning actions taken by Mr. Zaccaro when he was serving as an estate conservator constituted the bulk of the negative coverage (Blumenthal 1984; Roberts 1984). Though his actions were ultimately found to be legal, the public was left with the sense that something "shady" had gone on (Dowd 1984). Similarly, charges that her husband "had business dealings with purported organized crime figures" (Perlez 1984b) reminded readers of reports about Ferraro's parents being arrested for "running a numbers game" (Perlez 1984c).

While less intense, Palin also faced some negativity regarding her husband, Todd Palin. While the media spent some time discussing a drunk driving charge leveled against the "first dude," as he liked to be called, years earlier (Zernike and Severson 2008), they spent the most time reporting on his involvement in what became known as Troopergate. The press focused intensely on his refusal to cooperate with a legislative investigation into accusations that he had used his wife's authority as governor to pressure state employees to fire a state trooper, his former brother-in-law who had gone through a contentious divorce with his sister (Yardley 2008). Ultimately, the coverage worsened when the investigation concluded that the charges were founded, and that Governor Palin had "abused the powers of her office" by permitting her husband to use resources of her office to pressure for the state trooper's dismissal (Kovaleski 2008).

Clearly, the media provided the public with plenty of negative information about these candidates' spouses, but did it matter? While Ferraro and Palin were highly influential candidates, Quayle's 1992 impact on voters ranks him squarely in the middle of the pack. Overall then, the amount and negativity of media coverage of candidate marital status appears to be somewhat related to the impact that VP candidates had on voters, though this type of coverage proves to be less important than other types investigated.[10] The multivariate models presented in Table 5.6 emphasize this point. While the raw percentage of stories mentioning candidate marital status proves unrelated to VP impact, negativity with which candidates' marital statuses were mentioned appears to help explain why some VP candidates mean more to Independent voters than others. Candidates who received more negative coverage of their marriages appear to affect the votes of more Independent voters.[11]

Finally, with regard to media coverage of a candidate's race/ethnicity, we see that Geraldine Ferraro was the sole VP candidate to receive any mention of race and that she also exhibits a much larger impact on voters than all other VP candidates.[12] Even so, this relationship is likely spurious. The limited variation in the media coverage of race variable offers little analytical leverage, and the media mentions of race are highly correlated with the level and intensity of media coverage variables presented in chapter 3. Thus, it seems highly unlikely that this single, neutral, mention of race was the factor that explains why Ferraro resonated so much more with voters than other VP candidates. As we have seen previously, the other sorts of media attention that Ferraro attracted would be much more likely to explain her extraordinary impact on voters.

Table 5.6: Media Coverage of Candidate Marital Status and Vice Presidential Impact, 1972-2008

	I.	II.	III.
Percent of All Coverage Mentioning Candidate Marital Status	0.989	----	----
Percent of All Coverage Negatively Mentioning Candidate Marital Status	----	8.428 *	----
Percent of Mentions of Candidate Marital Status that are Negative	----	----	0.827 **
Presidential Approval	0.019	0.368	0.381
Economic Conditions	0.918	-0.517	-0.597
Constant	6.615	-8.815	-9.431
Number of Cases	20	20	20
Adjusted R-squared	0.029	0.119	0.137

Note: Cell entries are unstandardized OLS regression coefficients. Dependent variable is absolute value of "Percent of Independent Voters Affected" as reported in Figure 2.1.
*$p<0.010$; **$p<0.05$ (two-tailed).*

Overall, the data indicate that the media tend to focus on vice presidential candidate characteristics that make them unique in some way. The media tends to fixate on candidates breaking the mold of the typical male Protestant running mate and tends to discuss their unique characteristics more. Importantly, this media focus affects voters by highlighting key candidate characteristics linked to vote choice. When voters learn more about a candidate's sex and religious preference, and to a lesser degree, their marital status, they let their feelings about the candidate influence their vote choice more.

Summary

This chapter focused on the role that media coverage of candidate sociodemographic characteristics plays in making voters consider their feelings about some vice presidential candidates more than others. While candidate race likely played no role—and marital status played only a minor role in predicting which VP candidates affect voter decision making more – media coverage of candidate sex and religious preference helped to account for the large impact that the candidacies of Ferraro, Lieberman, and Palin had on voters. Overall, the findings suggest that media coverage of candidate characteristics account for some of the variation in VP impact over the past 40 years, but that some candidate characteristics matter more than others.

The next chapter moves beyond the influence of information about basic candidate characteristics to explore the ways in which media coverage of vice presidential candidates' job-related personality traits might influence the impact that these candidates have on voters. After reviewing reasons why voters are likely to pay more attention to information about key personality traits of candidates in presidential elections, I will test to see if media coverage of such vice presidential candidate traits helps to explain why some VP candidates matter more to voters than others.

Notes

[1] This mention was only a small part of a larger story on the Democratic Party's efforts to reach out to ethnic voters in Ohio.

[2] Percent of media coverage mentioning marital status: Gore, 1996 = 4.9; Edwards, 2004 = 5.2; Cheney, 2000 = 8.2; Ferraro, 1984 = 9.2; Quayle, 1992 = 9.5.

[3] When considering this measure of negativity, it is important to remember that this measure excludes all articles that do not mention the characteristic. Consequently, the raw number of articles on which the percentages presented is sometimes low.

[4] The bivariate correlation between overall coverage of sex and vice presidential impact on voters is 0.687 (p=0.000, two-tailed). The correlation between percent of all coverage that negatively mentions sex, as well as percent of all mentions of sex that are negative, and vice presidential impact is 0.715 (p=0.000, two-tailed).

[5] These results also hold when controls for the presidential media coverage, traits, and characteristics discussed in Chapter 3 are included.

[6] A test of the directional hypothesis that negative coverage of a vice presidential candidate's sex leads to less support for the that candidate's ticket confirms such a relationship. For Democratic vice presidential candidates, the more positively the candidate's sex is covered, the more likely Independent voters are to support that ticket (bivariate correlation between raw percent of Independent voters affected and positive coverage of candidate sex = +0.807, p=0.005). On the Republican side, more positive coverage of candidate sex is associated with less support for the Democratic ticket, and more support for the Republican ticket (correlation between raw percentage of Independent voters affected and positive coverage of candidate sex = -0.278, p=0.037).

[7] The bivariate correlation between overall coverage of religion and vice presidential impact on voters is 0.773 (p=0.000, two-tailed). The correlation between percent of all coverage that negatively mentions religion, as well as the percent of all mentions of religion that are negative, and vice presidential impact is 0.715 (p=0.000, two-tailed).

[8] A test of the directional hypothesis that negative coverage of a vice presidential candidate's religious preference leads to less support for the that candidate's ticket confirms such a relationship. For Democratic vice presidential

candidates, the more positively the candidate's religious preference is covered, the more likely Independent voters are to support that ticket (bivariate correlation between raw percent of Independent voters affected and positive coverage of candidate religious preference = +0.884, p=0.001). On the Republican side, more positive coverage of candidate religious preference is associated with less support for the Democratic ticket, and more support for the Republican ticket (correlation between raw percentage of Independent voters affected and positive coverage of candidate religious preference = -0.099, p=0.085).

[9] The bivariate correlation between overall coverage of marital status and vice presidential impact on voters is 0.310 (p=0.184, two-tailed).

[10] The correlation between percent of all coverage that negatively mentions marital status and vice presidential impact is 0.408 (p=0.074), and the correlation between the percent of all mentions of marital status that are negative and vice presidential impact is 0.424 (p=0.063, two-tailed).

[11] A test of the directional hypothesis that negative coverage of a vice presidential candidate marital status leads to less support for the candidate's ticket provides some support, though the results are statistically insignificant. For Democratic vice presidential candidates, the more positively the candidate's marital status is covered, the more likely Independent voters are to support that ticket (bivariate correlation between raw percent of Independent voters affected and positive coverage of candidate marital status = +0.413, p=0.235). On the Republican side, more positive coverage of candidate marital status is associated with less support for the Democratic ticket, and more support for the Republican ticket (correlation between raw percentage of Independent voters affected and positive coverage of candidate marital status = -0.282, p=0.429).

[12] The bivariate correlation between overall coverage of race and vice presidential impact on voters is 0.715 (p=0.000, two-tailed). The correlation between percent of all coverage that is negative and percent of coverage of race that is negative cannot be calculated since all race coverage of Ferraro was neutral.

6

How Media Coverage of Candidate Traits Matters

While the previous chapter revealed that voters tend to let their feelings about the candidates affect their vote choices more when the candidates receive more negative media coverage of certain personal characteristics, this chapter focuses on coverage of candidate personality traits. Just as voters look to candidates' sociodemographic characteristics to gain important information that will help them cast their ballots, they are also likely to use their impressions of candidates' personality traits to do so.

   This chapter asks if shining a light on vice presidential personality matters. It will investigate whether VP candidates receiving more media coverage, particularly more negative media coverage, of job-related personality traits impact voter decision making more than those who receive less (and less negative) coverage. After reviewing the reasons why candidate personality traits can influence voters, I construct measures capturing media coverage of these traits and illustrate how some vice presidential candidates receive more coverage of this sort than others. I then explore the relationship between such media coverage and VP impact on voters, finding that coverage of some traits matters more than others and that negative coverage matters more than positive or neutral coverage. Negative media coverage of candidates' political experience and intelligence appears to increase vice presidential impact on voters.

Spotlighting Candidate Personality

Just as candidates' sociodemographic characteristics carry messages to voters, so do their personality traits. Though some of the earliest and most influential voting models treated candidate characteristics as important (Campbell, Gurin, and Miller 1954; Campbell, et al. 1960), the role that personality traits play in voter decision making were not closely studied until more recently. Not surprisingly, voters tend to care most about candidate personality "focused around traits relevant to their roles as public representatives," (Funk 1996: 3) with four key candidate traits most closely associated to vote choice – competence, integrity, leadership ability, and empathic qualities (Kinder, 1983, 1986; Brady and Johnston, 1987). Though all four of these personality dimensions have been linked to voter decision making, competence and integrity assessments have repeatedly shown a stronger relationship with vote choice than leadership ability and empathy (Funk 1999; McCurley and Mondak 1995; Markus 1982; Miller and Miller 1976; Mondak 1995; Page 1978; Popkin 1991).

Researchers frequently measure voter perceptions of candidate competence with questions about whether voters view the candidate as hardworking, intelligent, and knowledgeable, and use voter assessments of candidate decency and morality to assess integrity (Pierce 1993). Judgments of these qualities frequently exhibit a strong influence on voter evaluations of political figures (Kinder, 1983, 1986; Kinder et al., 1980; Page, 1978; Miller and Miller, 1976; Miller, Wattenberg, and Malanchuk, 1986; Rahn et al., 1990), with voters often reporting their likes and dislikes of presidential candidates in terms of these traits (Funk 1996). While not showing as strong an impact, voter perceptions of candidate leadership ability and empathy also influence voter decision making. Researchers typically gauge leadership ability with questions about how inspiring the candidate is and whether the voter perceives the candidate as a strong leader, while empathy involves asking voters if they feel the candidate is compassionate, kind, or cares about people like the voter (Pierce 1993). Though voters rarely mention empathy concerns when evaluating politicians (Funk 1996: 3-4; see also Kinder et al., 1980; Miller, Wattenberg, and Malanchuk, 1986), empirical findings bear out the importance of empathy concerns in predicting vote choice (Bean 1993; Brown et al. 1988; Kinder 1986; Miller, Wattenberg, and Manchuk 1986). Accounting for these seemingly contradictory findings, Funk (1996) argues that empathy concerns may be important to voters but are simply consciously reported less often. Further, she points out the ways in which politicians frequently offer overt appeals in attempts to seem more "warm, sociable, and empathic" (Funk 1996: 4). Similarly, voter assessments of leadership traits show some relationship with voter decision making, though the impact pales in comparison to other traits (Kinder 1986; Miller and Miller 1976; Shanks and Miller 1990, 1991).

On the whole, candidate traits serve as a "major determinant of evaluations and vote choice" (Druckman and Parkin 2005: 1032; see also Funk 1999; Markus 1982, Rahn et al. 1990), and voter inferences about personality traits tend to dominate voter impressions of candidates (McGraw 2003: 398). Pierce (1993), for instance, found that once candidate traits were included in a model of vote choice, few issue considerations remained significant predictors. Hayes (2009) reports that candidate traits typically account for more than one-quarter of the open-ended responses voters offer when they are asked what they most like or dislike about candidates. It is, therefore, not surprising that a wealth of studies point to the significant and independent impact that voter perceptions of key personality traits have on vote choice since the 1950s (see e.g., Funk 1999; Hayes 2005, 2009; Kinder, et al 1980; Kinder 1986; Markus 1982; Miller and Miller 1976; Miller and Shanks 1996; Stokes 1966).

Given the prominent role the media plays in bringing candidates to the public, it is perhaps no surprise that researchers have documented evidence of media effects with regard to candidate traits. By focusing on candidate image, the media primes voters to make "personal attributes a central component of political evaluation" (Hayes 2009: 233; see also Funk 1996). As the media pays more attention to candidate's personality, key candidate traits become more accessible in the public's mind and subsequently weigh more heavily in their vote choice (Druckman 2004; Druckman et al. 2004; Hayes 2009; Jacobs and Shapiro 1994). Even very small changes in the portrayal of candidate traits affect voter decision making (Druckman and Parkin 2005: 1032); and campaign professionals, realizing this, concern themselves greatly with the ways in which the media portrays their candidates (see Funk 1999: 700). Not only does media attention to personality traits make them more important to voters, this effect sustains itself over time. "Once formed, trait judgments about others tend to last in memory long after the details on which they were based have been forgotten" (Funk 1996: 1). Consequently, the increased importance of personality traits created by the media likely sticks with voters as they enter the voting booth.

As with sociodemographic characteristics, I expect that when the media focuses more attention on vice presidential candidates' personality traits, these candidates will come to more heavily impact vote choice. Once again, the candidates who are most negatively covered are expected to exert the greatest impact. Given the relatively weaker impact that leadership and empathy concerns have shown in the past, I also expect media coverage of these characteristics to play smaller, if any, roles in explaining the impact that vice presidential candidates have on vote choice.

Measuring Candidate Traits

Following the procedure used in the previous chapter, I use the random sample of articles written about presidential campaign candidates (see Appendix B for details on sampling and coding procedures) to measure the volume and tone of articles written about seven candidate traits – political experience, intelligence, honesty, morality, leadership, inspiration, and compassion. These traits capture the four important trait dimensions identified by the literature. Mentions of candidates' leadership and inspiration capture the leadership component; coverage of candidate intelligence and political experience represent the competence dimension; stories about morality and honesty correspond to the integrity factor; and compassion serves as a measure of empathy. Each of the selected stories about vice presidential candidates was first coded to indicate which, if any, of the traits were mentioned. As in the previous chapter, any reference to one of the candidate traits under examination was noted, regardless of the context within which it was mentioned. Then each story that mentioned a trait was scored to indicate whether the coverage of that trait was negative (coded 1), neutral/balanced (coded 2), or positive (coded 3). Taking the political experience trait as an example, positive codings went to stories like the one that called Joe Biden an "astute politician" (Broder 2008). In contrast, negative ratings went to stories such as the ones calling Palin "unsophisticated" (Powell 2008) or quoting a source calling her "a bucket of fluff" (Leibovich 2008a). Meanwhile stories that simply referred to their previously held offices were coded as neutral. Coding decisions were made similarly for the remaining traits.

Volume of Media Coverage of Candidate Traits

The media treats presidential and vice presidential candidates relatively evenly when it comes to discussing their office-related personality traits. Overall volume of media mentions for all seven of the traits reported on Table 6.1 are roughly equivalent for presidential and vice presidential candidates. Political experience was by far the most commonly mentioned candidate trait, with an average of more than half of all coverage of presidential candidates and almost half of all coverage of vice presidential candidates mentioning this trait. Leadership ranks as the second most covered trait, with about 13% of all coverage of candidates, presidential and vice presidential alike, mentioning candidates' ability to be a strong leader for the nation.

Table 6.1: Volume of Media Coverage of Candidate Personality Traits

	Vice Presidential Candidates			Presidential Candidates		
	Minimum	Maximum	Mean (Std. Dev.)	Minimum	Maximum	Mean (Std. Dev.)
Political Experience	4.7	90.4	49.16 (25.84)	0.0	92.5	57.84 (30.39)
Intelligence	0.9	13.9	5.31 (3.09)	0.0	11.0	2.50 (2.86)
Honesty	0.0	15.1	4.56 (3.58)	0.0	11.0	3.44 (3.05)
Morality	0.0	12.9	4.68 (3.26)	0.0	20.8	4.13 (4.75)
Leadership	1.4	37.6	12.89 (8.82)	0.0	28.6	13.38 (8.49)
Inspiration	1.4	12.9	5.62 (2.84)	2.0	12.1	6.44 (2.99)
Compassion	0.0	5.7	2.02 (1.63)	0.0	10.4	2.64 (2.39)

Note: Cell entries are percent of all media coverage mentioning candidate that discuss the trai.t

Intelligence rates as the least mentioned presidential trait in media coverage, with only 2.5% of all stories mentioning presidential intelligence. At the same time, the media devoted more than 5.3% of their stories to discussing the intelligence of vice presidential candidates. The media's focus on Sarah Palin's intelligence during the 2008 campaign largely explains this difference. As further discussed below, almost 14% of all media coverage of her candidacy mentioned her intelligence, typically in a negative manner.

Negativity of Media Coverage of Candidate Traits

The media appear to turn negative much more often with regard to vice presidential candidate traits than they did with regard to candidate sociodemographic characteristics. While the media typically discussed candidates' personality traits in a negative manner less than six percent of the time, the first set of columns on Table 6.2 shows some traits draw more negative attention than others. The media tends to focus a good deal of negative energy toward discussing the leadership abilities of some VP candidates while almost never negatively presenting the candidates' compassion. A much higher level of negativity emerges, however, when we look only at stories mentioning each characteristic. As the second set of columns on Table 6.2 illustrates, on average, nearly 40% of media coverage concerning VP intelligence, honesty, and leadership ability turns negative. Further, more than one-quarter of the media's attention to candidates' morality and inspirational ability—and almost one-fifth of the media mentions of candidate compassion—takes a negative tone. [1]

Table 6.2: Negativity of Media Coverage of Vice Presidential Candidate Personality Traits

	Percent of All Coverage that Negatively Mentions Trait			Percent of Mentions of Trait that are Negative		
	Minimum	Maximum	Mean (Std. Dev.)	Minimum	Maximum	Mean (Std. Dev.)
Political Experience	0.0	12.9	2.96 (3.36)	0.0	30.0	7.12 (8.46)
Intelligence	0.0	11.9	2.47 (2.86)	0.0	85.7	39.74 (27.14)
Honesty	0.0	11.8	2.34 (2.81)	0.0	78.6	37.62 (23.45)
Morality	0.0	9.7	1.85 (2.53)	0.0	83.3	26.29 (27.53)
Leadership	0.0	23.7	5.79 (6.06)	0.0	75.0	37.08 (27.62)
Inspiration	0.0	8.6	2.07 (2.28)	0.0	66.7	31.13 (25.39)
Compassion	0.0	3.6	0.50 (0.93)	0.0	75.0	18.75 (27.48)

Again there is evidence that some candidates are treated more harshly than others. For each candidate characteristic, there was at least one VP candidate who entirely escaped negative media coverage while others endured between 30% and almost 86% negative coverage. For example, while 30% of the media attention to Dan Quayle's political experience was negative, the political experience of George H.W. Bush (in both 1980 and 1984) and Spiro Agnew (in 1972) went unassailed. Similarly, while nearly 86% of the media coverage mentioning Palin's intelligence discussed it in a negative manner, the intelligence of eight other VP candidates went unquestioned by the media.

Media Coverage of Candidate Traits and Vice Presidential Impact

To explore the possibility that media coverage of key candidate traits makes them more important to voters, I examined the relationship between coverage of the seven different candidate traits and the impact that vice presidential candidates have on voters. Table 6.3 summarizes the relationships between the different traits and VP impact. As this table reveals, the overall volume of trait-related media coverage proves to be unrelated to VP impact on voters for all seven traits. It does not appear that VP candidates who receive more media attention to their job-related traits more strongly impact voter decision making.

Table 6.3: Media Coverage of Vice Presidential Candidate Personality Traits and Vice Presidential Impact on Independent Voters, 1972-2008

	% of All Coverage Mentioning Trait	% of All Coverage that Negatively Mentions Trait	% of Mentions of Trait that are Negative
Political Experience	-0.125	0.118	**0.427**
	(0.601)	(0.621)	**(0.060)**
Intelligence	-0.023	0.191	**0.445**
	(0.923)	(0.421)	**(0.050)**
Honesty	-0.01	-0.027	0.28
	0.967	0.91	0.378
Morality	0.017	-0.06	0.068
	(0.943)	(0.803)	(0.774)
Leadership Ability	0.096	0.167	0.311
	(0.688)	(0.481)	(0.182)
Inspirational Ability	0.191	0.312	0.232
	(0.419)	(0.181)	(0.324)
Compassion	0.093	0.15	0.207
	(0.695)	(0.527)	(0.382)

Note: Cell entries are Pearson's r bivariate correlations and statistical significance (in parentheses). All statistical tests are two-tailed. Entries in bold are statistically significant at p< 0.10 (two-tailed).

This does not mean that media attention to these traits is wholly unimportant, however. Focusing only on stories that mention candidate traits, the last column of Table 6.3 reveals that vice presidential candidates who receive more negative media coverage of their political experience and intelligence exert a stronger impact on voters. The positive correlation coefficients reported here indicate that the more a trait is negatively mentioned, the more impact VP candidates exert on voters. As Figure 6.1 illustrates, two of the most influential vice presidential candidates of the past forty years, Ferraro and Palin, received a very high degree of negative media attention to their political experience. About 21% of the time the media discussed each of these candidates' political experience, they did so negatively. The press particularly hammered on both candidates' scant foreign policy experience. Ferraro's lack of the "kind of broad experience in government, especially in foreign policy, that Mr. Bush [, her Republican vice-presidential counterpart, had] on his resume"(Gailey

Figure 6.1: Negative Mentions of Vice Presidential Political Experience and Vice Presidential Impact on Independent Voters, 1972-2008

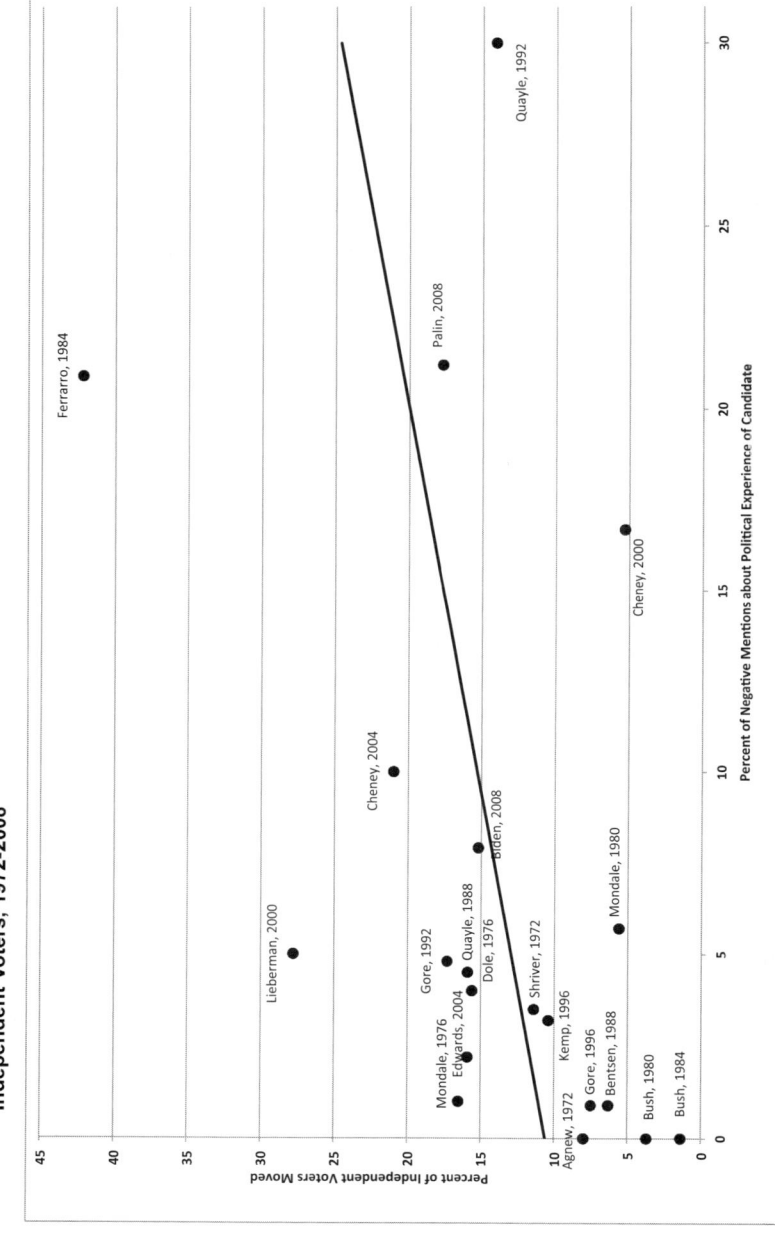

Note: Percent of negative mentions as reported in Table 6.2. Percent of Independent voters affected is absolute value of percent reported in Figure 2.1. The bivariate correlation for this relationship is 0.427 (p=0.060, two-tailed).

1984) led to much criticism. The attacks were so strong, in fact, that Ferraro told then popular daytime talk show host Phil Donahue that she felt as though she was going through a "doctoral testing process as every single reporter wanted to know how much [she] knew about foreign policy and arms control" (Perlez 1984e). Palin received even harsher treatment. Concerns about her political experience combined with negative impressions about her intelligence (see below) casting doubt on her ability to perform as vice president—let alone president—should the time come. Calling her "a walking affront to the many Republican women (not to mention women in general) who are, in fact, qualified to hold the highest office in the land" (Herbert 2008a), the media led many voters to question whether she possessed the requisite political experience to assume the position she was seeking. Reports often quoted potential voters expressing "[worry] about Ms. Palin's lack of experience" (Philips 2008), being "turned off by Ms. Palin" because she was "too inexperienced to be president" (Silverman 2008), and "living in fear of a Palin presidency" (Capuzzo 2008).

Not to be outdone, Dan Quayle's political experience received negative coverage 30% of the time it was mentioned by the press in the 1992 campaign, perhaps accounting for his ability to influence the votes of more than 14% of Independent voters that year. Quayle had "been a magnet for criticism since George Bush chose him as a running mate in 1988" (Apple 1991). Negative coverage of his, and his wife's, public statements regarding family values drew harsh criticism during his first term in office (see Chapter 5 for details), and any concerns the public had about his ability to assume the presidency were brought to the forefront when President Bush suffered an irregular heartbeat during an afternoon jog. Just months before the 1992 general election campaign kicked off, the public was confronted with the real possibility of waking up to an America with President Quayle in charge. During his first term, Quayle had made little ground in "refuting the widespread view that he is terribly inadequate to the challenges of the presidency" (Chicago Tribune 1991). As the media reported, "The instant the news about President Bush's heart problem came through, Mr. Quayle's name flashed into everybody's mind. For a lot of Americans it was followed immediately by three words: 'Oh, my God'" (Rosenthal 1991). It was no wonder, then, that during the 1992 campaign, "Quayle's approval rating remain[ed] abysmally low" and "the vice president [had become] inextricably identified with all things negative," (Hanlin 1991) especially questions about whether he had the necessary political experience to become Commander in Chief.

A similar story plays out in Figure 6.2, which reveals that the four most influential vice presidential candidates of the past four decades receive high levels of media negativity when it comes to their intelligence. The media thrashed Sarah Palin, with nearly 86% of media mentions about her intelligence going negative. Perhaps the kindest thing the media uttered about Palin's intelligence was that she showed a "lack of familiarity with major national or international issues" (Draper 2008). More often she was painted as "being essentially unserious and uncurious" (Leibovich 2008b). As *Wall Street Journal* columnist Peggy Noonan put it, "She doesn't think aloud. She just ...says things" (Noonan 2008). Media criticism of Palin's intellectual capacity ramped up following her now infamous television interview with Charles Gibson early in the campaign season. Following the interview, journalists concluded that Palin did not "appear to understand some of the most important issues" confronting the nation (Herbert 2008b). From seemingly being stumped by what the "Bush Doctrine" was to claiming that she had special insight into Russian actions against neighboring Georgia because "you can actually see Russia from land here in Alaska," (ABC News 2009) her interviews led the media to wonder whether Palin lacked the intellectual capacity to be the nation's number two. Only days after the Gibson interview, *Saturday Night Live* immortalized Palin's gaffes when Tina Fey, portraying Palin, spoofed the candidate's remark by saying "I can see Russia from my house." The mainstream media repeatedly mentioned Fey's impersonation, further cementing the impression of Palin's unintelligence in the public's mind. Given this level of negative attention, it is perhaps not surprising that she influenced the votes of nearly 18% of Independent voters in the 2008 election.

Similarly, 60% of the time the media discussed Dick Cheney's intelligence during the 2004 campaign, they did so in a negative manner, while about 58% of the time they questioned Ferraro's intelligence. The media questioned Cheney's intelligence regarding his assertions that Iraq was developing a nuclear weapon, that it was a place for terrorists to get illicit weapons (Krugman 2004), that American involvement in Iraq was "a great success story" (Dowd 2004), as well as accusing him of "misreading the nature of the 2001 California energy crisis" (Krugman 2004). For Ferraro, her campaign gaffes, such as confusing the terms "first use and first strike" in a statement about the use of nuclear weapons (Mohr 1984), led the media to question her intellectual capacity on a number of occasions.

The multivariate analyses presented in Table 6.4 further illustrate the importance of candidate intelligence and political experience in ex-

Figure 6.2 Negative Mentions of Vice Presidential Intelligence and Vice Presidential Impact on Independent Voters, 1972-2008

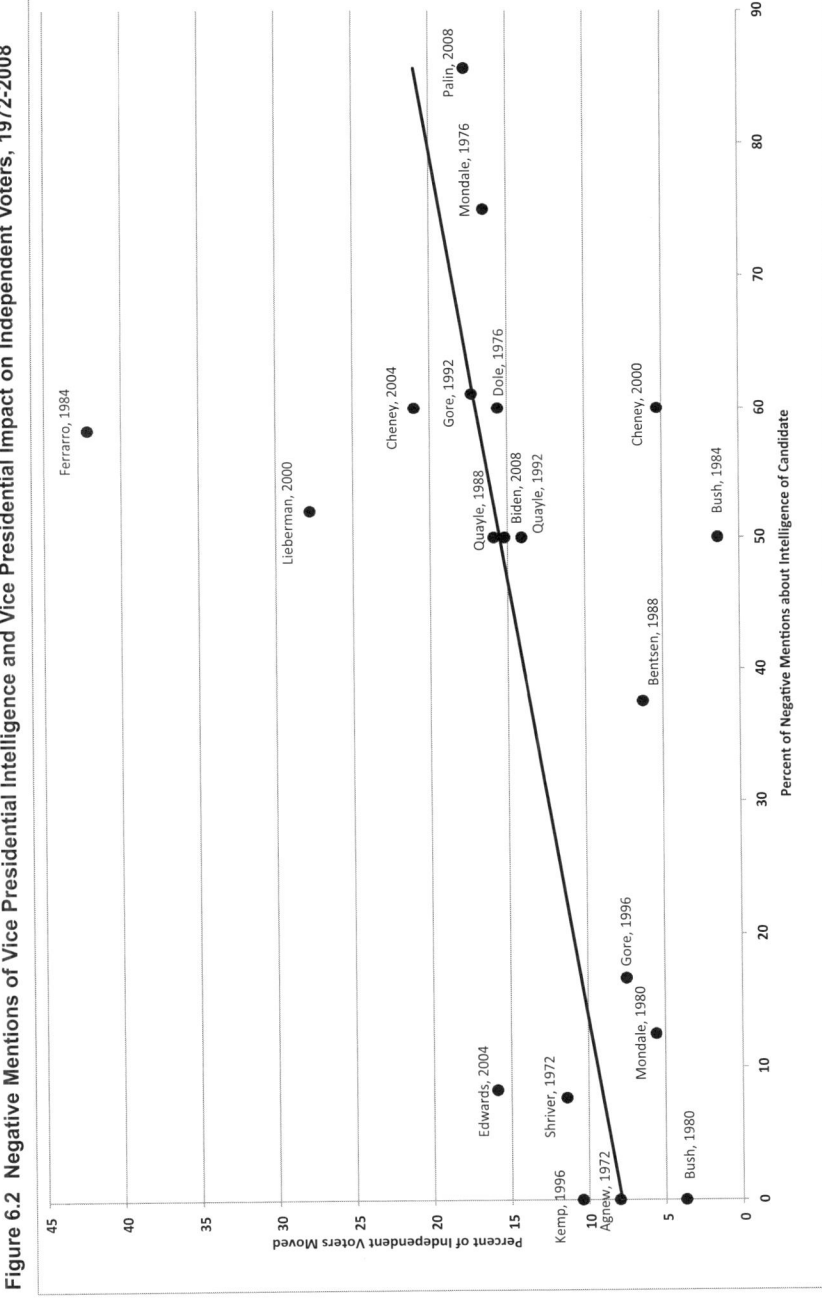

Note: Percent of negative mentions as reported in Table 6.2. Percent of Independent voters affected is absolute value of percent reported in Figure 2.1. The bivariate correlation for this relationship is 0.445 (p=0.050, two-tailed).

plaining why some VP candidates have a greater impact on Independent voters than others.[2] Candidates who receive more negative coverage of their political experience or intelligence exhibit a greater impact on Independent voters, and negative coverage of political experience seems to play the largest role. Each additional percent of negative media coverage of a candidate's political experience affects a little more than one-half of one percent of Independent voters. At the same time, each additional percent of negative media coverage of candidates' intelligence affects only about two-tenths of one percent of Independent voters.[3]

Table 6.4: Media Coverage of Candidate Traits and Vice Presidential Impact, 1972-2008

	I.	II.
Percent of Negative Mentions about Candidate Political Experience	0.548 **	----
Percent of Negative Mentions about Candidate Intelligence	----	0.157 *
Presidential Approval	0.190	0.109
Economic Conditions	0.300	0.337
Constant	-1.986	0.446
Number of Cases	20	20
Adjusted R-squared	0.125	0.101

Note: Cell entries are unstandardized OLS regression coefficients. Dependent variable is absolute value of "Percent of Independent Voters Affected". *p<0.010; **p<0.05 (two-tailed).

So while voters do not appear to consider all job-related candidate traits, they do seem persuaded by media coverage of candidates' competence. When vice presidential candidates receive more negative media coverage of their intelligence and political experience they exhibit a stronger impact on voters. Voters, it appears, pay more attention to the VP candidates when they have concerns about their abilities to assume the presidency if called upon. This finding fits well with previous research showing competence concerns to be more important than leadership and empathy concerns. Taken with the findings from the previous chapters, these results help further explain why some VP candidates matter more to voters than others.

Summary

This chapter focused on the role that media coverage of candidate personality traits plays in making voters consider their feelings about some vice presidential candidates more than others. The analyses examined media coverage of seven important job-related traits – political experience, intelligence, honesty, morality, leadership, inspiration, and compassion. Findings revealed that some personality traits matter more to voters than others, and negative coverage of some traits matters more. Only negative coverage of candidates' political experience and intelligence help explain why some VP candidates affect more voters than others. Overall, the findings suggest that media coverage of candidate traits can account for some of the variation in VP impact, but that some candidate personality traits matter more than others.

Along with previous chapters, these findings further clarify potential reasons why some VP candidates affect voters more than others. The next chapter pulls all these findings together. I first review what the key findings and non-findings from previous chapters tell us about the historical importance of VP candidates in elections. Next I explain what these findings tell us about why four candidates – Geraldine Ferraro, Joseph Lieberman, Sarah Palin, and Dick Cheney (in 2004) – affected voters more than other candidates. Finally, I conclude by considering the likely role of VP candidates in future elections.

Notes

[1] As in the previous chapter, it is important to remember that this measure excludes all articles that do not mention the trait so the raw number of articles on which the percentages presented is sometimes low.

[2] These results also hold when controls for the presidential media coverage, traits, and characteristics discussed in Chapter 3 are included.

[3] A test of the directional hypothesis that negative coverage of a vice presidential traits leads to less support for that candidate's ticket confirms such a relationship. For Democratic vice presidential candidates, the more positively the candidate's political experience and intelligence are covered, the more likely Independent voters are to support that ticket (bivariate correlation between raw percent of Independent voters affected and % positive mentions of political experience = +0.809, p=0.005; correlation between voters affected and % positive mentions of intelligence = +0.533, p=0.103). On the Republican side, more positive coverage of candidate political experience, honesty, and intelligence is associated with less support for the Democratic ticket, and more support for the Republican ticket (correlation between raw percentage of Independent voters affected and positive coverage of candidate political

experience = -0.409, p=0.040; correlation between voters affected and % positive mentions of intelligence = -0.500, p=0.104).

7

The Performance of
Second Fiddles

The research presented in the previous chapters illustrated the variable impact vice presidential candidates have had on vote choice since the 1970s and revealed the important role the media plays in explaining why some second fiddles mean more to voters than others. In this chapter, I first discuss the historical importance of vice presidential candidates in elections of the past four decades by reviewing the key findings and non-findings from the previous chapters. Then, after more closely examining the reasons why four vice presidential candidates proved to be much more important to voters than others, I speculate about the role that vice presidential candidates will likely play in future elections.

Who's Listening to Second Fiddles and Why?

The findings presented in this book suggest that even though many vice presidential candidates mean very little to voters, there are instances when those occupying the bottom of the ticket can affect voter decision making. Importantly, however, these candidates do not affect all voters in the same manner. As Chapter 2 illustrated, feelings about VP candidates exhibit remarkably little, if any, impact on voters with pre-existing partisan allegiances. Self-proclaimed Democrats and Republicans seldom let their feelings about the bottom of the ticket affect their vote choice. In contrast, those without a partisan anchor tend to bring their impressions of VP candidates into the voting booth. Since 1970, an average of about 14% of all Independent voters were persuaded to support one party's ticket over the other because of their feelings about VP candidates. Even among these voters, though, not every VP candidate makes an impact. Some vice presidential candidates matter more to voters than others. While Geraldine Ferraro (1984) influenced the votes of more than 42% of Independent voters, her Republican counterpart in that election, George H.W. Bush, affected less than 2% of these voters.

The varied impact of VP candidates can be explained, at least in part, by the nature of the media attention given to them. Confirming much of the existing research about the importance of media priming effects in electoral behavior, Chapter 3 revealed that VP candidates receiving more—and more intense—media coverage tend to exert much more influence over the vote choices of Independents. As some have suggested, the media can influence the factors that citizens consider when making political decisions (Kelleher and Wolack 2006). And the results here suggest the media can prime voters to consider their feelings about vice presidential candidates in much the same way they influence voters to consider certain issues or candidate traits (e.g., Druckman 2004; Druckman and Holmes 204; Funk 1999; Hetherington 1996; Jacobs and Shapiro 1994; Krosnick and Brannon 1993; McGraw and Ling 2003; Mendelsohn 1996).

Despite the many arguments that negative information should resonate more with voters (Fiske 1980; Hamilton and Zanna 1974; Johnson and Copeland 1989; Lau 1985 Kahn and Kenney 2004), Chapter 4 demonstrated that the negativity of the media coverage garnered by VP candidates during the general election campaign played little role in predicting which candidates make the greatest impact on voters. At the same time, however, the predicted negativity effects arose when examining incumbent vice presidential candidates. Incumbent vice presidents who were cast in a negative light during their first terms in office tended to have more impact on voters at reelectoin time. The high levels of media negativity targeted at incumbent VP candidate Dick Cheney proved especially telling on this point. Affecting only about 5% of Independent voters in the 2000 election, Cheney endured more than his share of negative media attention during his first term in office and subsequently swayed the votes of more than 20% of these voters during his 2004 re-election bid.

Moving beyond the volume and tone of media coverage, Chapter 5 illustrated how heightened media coverage of certain candidate characteristics can lead voters to contemplate their feelings about vice presidential candidates while in the voting booth. Just as many have illustrated the importance of candidate gender (Huddy and Terkildsen 1993; Leeper 1991; Kahn 1994; Matland 1994; Rosenwasser and Seale 1988; Sanbomatsu 2002; Sapiro 1981-82) and religion (McDermott 2009; Berinsky and Mendelberg 2005) in voter decision making, the analyses in this chapter revealed that heightened coverage related to a candidate's sex and religious preference (and to a lesser extent their marriages) increases the likelihood that voters will allow their feelings about the candidate to influence their vote choices. Further, the results confirmed the expected negativity bias with regard to media coverage of these candidate characteristics, especially when it came to vice presidential candidate Geraldine Ferraro. The most influential of all VP candidates, she also proved to be the only candidate who received negative coverage of her sex and religious preference, and endured the second most negative coverge of her marriage.

Finally, Chapter 6 echoed a long line of literature suggesting that candidate traits, particularly candidate competence, play a role in voter decision making (Funk 1999; McCurley and Mondak 1995; Markus 1982; Miller and Miller 1976; Mondak 1995; Page 1978; Popkin 1991). Again the results confirmed the importance of negative information. When the media focused more on the competence of vice presidential candidates, especially when they did so in a negative manner, voters were more likely to allow their feelings toward vice presidential candidates to influence their votes. Negative media attention to candidates' political experience and intelligence led some VP candidates to influence voters more than others, and it plays an important role in explaining the large impact of the Ferraro and Palin candidacies.

While these results provide some insight into the variable impact that VP candidates have on voters, it is important to consider three key limitations of these analyses. Two limitations concern the research design of this study. First, this investigation focuses on only the past 40 years. Though it seems unlikely, it is possible that elections during this period significantly differ from elections of earlier years. Certainly, the media has come to play a larger role in modern presidential elections, and perhaps this accounts for some of the findings of this book. Since the media shows no signs of losing its relevance in American politics, it is unlikely the importance of the findings presented here will become irrelevant in future elections. A second limitation of the analyses presetned in this book concerns the use of a single media outlet, the *New York Times*, as a source of information on media coverage of vice presidential candidates. As discussed in Chapter 3, even though the *New York Times* probably does not represent the information source for the typical voter, it is a reasonable proxy of the media messages reaching voters during presidential campaigns (Bartels 1996; Lau and Pomper 2004: 134; see also Druckman 2004) and is often used in studies of national elections (e.g., Ansolabehere, et al 1994; Franklin 1991; Holian 2004; Kelleher and Wolak 2006; Lau and Pomper 2004). Still, it might strengthen the analyses if additional media content measures, especially television coverage of candidates, were included.

The third concern lies with the way in which outliers might be affecting the results presented here. An outlier is a case that is numerically distant from the rest of the cases. That is, the case has a value far higher or far lower than most other cases in the dataset. For instance, a 65 year old student in a classroom of otherwise traditionally aged undergraduate students represents an outlier on the measure of age. Outliers can be problematic because they can cause statistical tests to exaggerate the strength relationships between variables. In the analyses presented here, a number of outliers exist and probably did influence the magnitude of some of the statistical results. For instance, Ferraro's extremely high impact score of 42.2 designates her as an outlier among the set of vice presidential candidates examined here. Similarly, the extreme volume of media coverage given to Palin (21.39% of all media coverage of candidates in the 2008 election) makes her an outlier on this measure.[1] Methods exist for dealing with the troublesome impact of outliers. Unfortunately, the most common tactic – simply ignoring them – is not appropriate here. While the presence of such cases certainly increases the value of the correlation and regression coefficients presented in this book, these cases represent precisely the cases I am seeking to explain. Why is it that Ferraro exhibited such a high impact or that the media became so enamored with Palin? If these outlying cases were removed, there would be no way to see that Ferraro probably impacted voters so strongly because the media focused on her much more intensely and negatively than on other candidates or that it was likely the negative media attention to Palin's intelligence and political experience, rather than her sex, that caused her to resonate more strongly with voters. Consequently, the outliers remain in the data and readers should take the magnitude of the statistical results reported here with caution.

Spotlighting Second Fiddles of the Past

The important role of media coverage illustrated in the previous chapters helps to explain why Geraldine Ferraro (1984), Joe Lieberman (1992), Dick Cheney (2004), and Sarah Palin (2008) were more meaningful to Independent voters than other vice presidential candidates. The large volume and intensity of media coverage focused on Geraldine Ferraro allowed her to sway the votes of more than 42% of Independent voters. As Table 7.1 illustrates, Ferraro received the most intense media coverage of all vice presidential candidates since 1972. Additionally, she received the most coverage—and most negative coverage—related to her sex and religious preference. While Palin received the second most coverage about her sex, the sheer volume of media attention focused on her, particularly her marriage, explains why she influenced the votes of nearly 18% of Independent voters. Similarly, she received the most—and the most negative—coverage of her intelligence and the second most negative coverage of her political experience. A focus on Lieberman's political experience played a role in his ability to sway nearly 28% of Independent voters, but attention to his Jewish religious heritage and negatively toned stories about his marriage also played important roles.

Table 7.1: Media Coverage of the Four Most Influential Vice Presidential Candidates

	Mean V.P. Candidate	Ferraro (1984)		Lieberman (2000)		Cheney (2004)		Palin (2008)	
	Score	Score	Rank	Score	Rank	Score	Rank	Score	Rank
Volume of Media Coverage	8.40	12.20	3rd	11.50	4th	7.50	12th	21.40	1st
Intensity of Media Coverage	1.42	1.68	1st	1.41	12th	1.38	14th	1.55	4th
% Moderate Coverage	15.70	22.30	3rd	20.40	7th	18.30	9th	21.90	5th
Overall Tone of Media Coverage	1.99	2.00	7th	1.94	18th	1.96	17th	1.88	20th
Candidate Image in Media Coverage	1.95	2.03	7th	1.78	18th	1.79	17th	1.74	20th
Media Coverage of Gender									
Volume of Coverage	2.23	28.50	1st	0.00	----	0.00	----	12.90	2nd
Negativity of Coverage	0.14	2.70	1st	0.00	----	0.00	----	0.00	----
Media Coverage of Religion									
Volume of Coverage	2.25	15.40	1st	14.30	2nd	1.10	8th	4.00	4th
Negativity of Coverage	0.25	5.00	1st	0.00	----	0.00	----	0.00	----
Media Coverage of Marital Status									
Volume of Coverage	4.25	9.20	4th	3.10	11th	3.20	10th	12.40	1st
Negativity of Coverage	2.29	16.70	2nd	0.00	----	0.00	----	4.00	3rd
Media Coverage of Political Experience									
Volume of Coverage	49.16	16.30	18th	86.60	2nd	28.60	15th	49.30	10th
Negativity of Coverage	7.12	20.90	3rd	5.00	8th	10.00	5th	21.20	2nd
Media Coverage of Honesty									
Volume of Coverage	4.56	5.30	3rd	6.00	6th	2.90	13th	7.00	5th
Negativity of Coverage	37.62	50.00	7th	78.60	1st	50.00	7th	50.00	7th
Media Coverage of Intelligence									
Volume of Coverage	5.31	4.60	13th	4.70	11th	7.10	4th	13.90	1st
Negativity of Coverage	39.74	58.30	5th	52.00	6th	60.00	4th	85.70	1st

Given the uniqueness of a female vice presidential candidate, it is perhaps no surprise that media coverage of Ferraro and Palin frequently focused on their sex or that the non-Protestant candidacies of Lieberman and Ferraro drew stories about their religious preferences. With the novelty of these candidates and the degree to which the media spotlight shined on them, Independent voters came to know these candidates better and subsequently take their feelings about them into account in the voting booth. Dick Cheney's ability to influence the votes of more than one in five Independent voters in the 2004 election presents more of a puzzle. Cheney, presenting the much more traditional image of an Anglo male vice presidential candidate with solid political experience, would be expected to garner little media attention and consequently play little role in voter decision making. While Cheney represented the typical vice presidential candidate in most ways, he did break with the tradition of vice presidents playing a background role in administrative decisions. Instead, he publicly took the lead on a number of important issues during his first term in office, something that had become obvious to voters by 2004. And while media coverage of Cheney during the 2004 campaign does little to explain the impact he exhibited on voters in that election, media coverage of his first term in office strongly predicts his impact on voters. Nearly 38% of the time the media mentioned Cheney during his first term in office, they did so in a negative manner. Voters appear to have formed impressions of him over the course of his first term in office and carried these feelings with them to the voting booth in 2004.

The Continuing Importance of Second Fiddles

While the effect that vice presidential candidates can have on the voting preferences of Independents is impressive, their impact on election outcomes likely remains fairly low. Because Independent voters typically constitute a rather small portion of the electorate, the aggregate impact that feelings about vice presidential candidates exert remains marginal. Since the early 1970s, purely Independent voters have comprised between seven and eighteen percent of all voters, with an average of 13% of voters identifying as Independent over this period. Thus, the impact that vice presidential candidates are likely to have on the general election outcome usually remains fairly low. In fact, as illustrated in Figure 7.1, since the 1970s, vice presidential candidates appear to be responsible for affecting the votes of less just 1.75% of the entire electorate in a typical election.[2] Though this impact is limited, it is important to realize that feelings about presidential candidates exert similarly small, though comparatively stronger, influence. Over the entire 1972-2008 period, feelings about the typical presidential candidates affected only about 4.25% of all voters.[3] As many in of those in the "minimal impact" school of thought suggest, longer-term factors tend to play vital roles in voter decision making and any single aspect of the campaign will likely play a small, though possibly important, part.

Figure 7.1 Percent of All Voters Affected by Increase in VP Candidate Ratings, 1972-2008

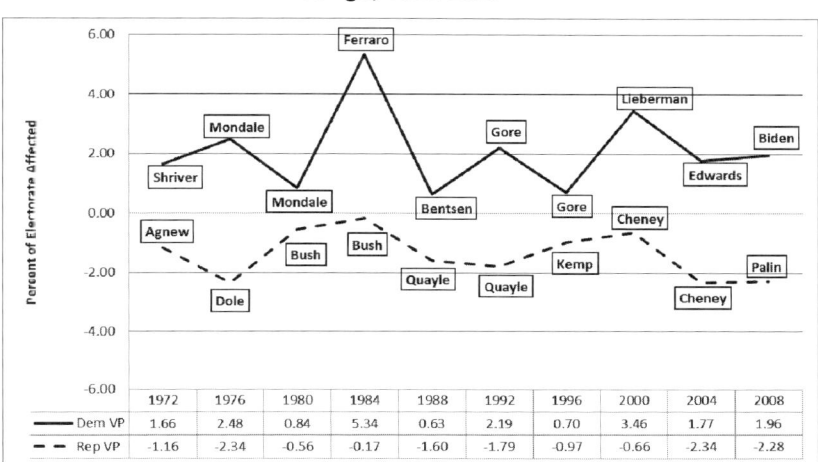

	1972	1976	1980	1984	1988	1992	1996	2000	2004	2008
Dem VP	1.66	2.48	0.84	5.34	0.63	2.19	0.70	3.46	1.77	1.96
Rep VP	-1.16	-2.34	-0.56	-0.17	-1.60	-1.79	-0.97	-0.66	-2.34	-2.28

Note: Vertical axis represents the change in percent of all voters expressing a preference for Democratic candidate.

Further, in years when VP candidates receive heightened media attention, their impacts are stronger. For instance, feelings about Geraldine Ferraro affected about 5.3% of the entire electorate in 1984, voter assessments of Lieberman impacted about 3.5% of all voters, and impressions of both Sarah Palin and Dick Cheney affected about 2.3% of the entire electorate. Considering the close vote margins in recent presidential elections, a vice presidential impact of similar magnitude could mean the difference in an election. Since 1972, the average nation-wide popular vote margin has been about 8.5%, and three presidential elections since 1972 have been decided by national popular vote margins of less than three percent.[4]

When it comes to the Electoral College, the results are even more striking. Over the past forty years, many states have witnessed popular vote margins smaller than the typical VP impact. While the typical vice president impacts the votes of about 1.75% of the electorate, 37 states since 1972 have witnessed victory margins of less than 1.7%. Therefore it is possible that feelings about vice presidential candidates could have changed the electoral vote distribution in at least 37 states over the past forty years. In two of those years, 1976 and 2000, the number of electoral votes potentially influenced by feelings about vice presidential candidates proves larger than the margin of victory in the Electoral

College. In 1976, eight states holding 78 electoral votes were decided by popular vote margins of less than 1.7%. The Electoral College vote in that year saw Jimmy Carter win by only a 57 vote margin. In 2000, when George W. Bush's Electoral College victory margin was only five votes, six states holding 59 electoral votes were decided by vote margins of less than 1.7% of the popular vote. Thus, in at least these two elections the feelings about a typical vice presidential candidate might have changed the election outcome.[5] So while the absolute impact vice presidential candidates have on election outcomes may be small, it could be consequential.

Further, it is possible that vice presidential candidates' impact may extend beyond Independent voters. Their impact may reverberate through other parts of the electorate, as well. The impact of some VP candidates may lie in their ability to mobilize the party's base. Many believe this is exactly the impact that Sarah Palin had in the 2008 election. Her nomination, some argued, "shore[d] up the conservative base" (Guerriero 2008) and spurred a "substantial jump in the percentage of Republicans saying they were more enthusiastic about voting in this election" (Gallup Poll 2008). Similarly, vice presidential candidates may make an impression on voters Hillygus and Shields (2008) identify as cross-pressured partisans. True partisans, these voters find appeal in a candidate from the other party on a single issue. For example, pro-choice Republicans may be drawn to support the Democratic ticket if targeted with the right appeals on this issue. Perhaps a vice presidential candidate's greatest impact may be in attracting such voters to the party's ticket. A vice presidential candidate might effectively communicate an issue-specific message to cross-pressured partisans that lures them to cast a ballot against their partisan allegiance. Before Mitt Romney had even clinched the Republican nomination, some suggested that he choose Brian Sandoval or Marco Rubio, both pro-choice candidates, as his running mate (Avlon 2012) with the possibility that some Democratic voters might be lured to support the Republican ticket by appeals from the bottom of the ticket on this issue.

The growing importance of vice presidential candidates in recent elections further suggests that voters are likely to let their feelings about them affect their vote choices in the future. The last three presidential races birthed three of the four most impactful vice presidential candidates since 1972. Lieberman's candidacy in 2000, Cheney's reelection in 2004, and Palin's bid in 2008 suggest vice presidential candidates might be playing more important electoral roles now than in the past. At the same time, it is important to remember that the media

[handwritten margin note:] appeal to a further wing of the party or moderate R + Ds who may switch based on an issue.

must choose to bring these candidates to the public's attention in order for them to matter, and that the media tend to be attracted to unique candidates. The past three vice presidential candidates each represent deviations from the "typical" vice presidential profile. The candidacy of Sarah Palin broke the traditional gender profile of vice presidents, Joe Lieberman provided the novelty of a Jewish vice president, and Dick Cheney's reelection bid brought a highly scrutinized incumbent vice president. This trend suggests that should a party choose a vice presidential nominee who is unique in some way, this candidate will likely spend a lot of time in the glare of the media spotlight. As a result, voters will probably take their feelings about this candidate into account more strongly come election day. Conversely, should both vice presidential candidates fit a more traditional mold, the media is less likely to spotlight them, making them less relevant to voters.

The likelihood of a party choosing a unique candidate may result from the strength of the opposing vice presidential candidate. The data on vice presidential impact over time indicate that in the years that vice presidential candidates exhibit strong impacts for one ticket (1984, 2000, 2008), the vice presidential candidate on the other party's ticket typically exerts comparatively little impact. Just as Palin's strong impact in 2008 juxtaposed Biden's typically lower impact, Cheney's impact in 2000 (when he faced Lieberman) and Bush's in 1984 (when he faced Ferraro) were diminished. In fact, the impact of Democratic and Republican vice presidential nominees proves to be negatively related, suggesting that when voters consider one vice presidential candidate in an election, the other is largely ignored.[6]

Perhaps this phenomenon derives from candidate strategy. A strong candidate on the bottom of one ticket might push the other party to field a unique vice presidential candidate in an attempt to garner media coverage and stimulate voter excitement. And the data offer some support of this contention. Media coverage of the parties' candidates is negatively related, suggesting that as the media spotlight shines on one candidate, the other is left in the shadows.[7] Whatever the electoral strategies might be, it remains clear that the selection of VP candidates will remain an important choice for presidential candidates and their campaign managers.

Tuning up for 2012

In fact, just one week into the 2012 election year, political pundits started forecasting the 2012 vice presidential nominees. Some suggested President Obama replace current vice president Joe Biden with Hillary

Clinton. Given the potentially tough re-election campaign that Obama faces and Biden's less than impressive impact on only 15% of Independent voters in the 2008 election, perhaps Clinton would "bring to [the] campaign a missing warmth and some of the voltage that has dissipated" during Obama's time in office (Keller 2012). And even before the Republican presidential nomination had been secured, speculation about a suitable VP candidate for presumptive nominee Mitt Romney flew. Some suggested Romney might do well to pick a vice-presidential candidate with a Hispanic background, such as Florida Senator, Marco Rubio (Parker 2012) as a means of appealing to important minority voters. Had either (or both) of these predictions come to fruition, it would have been likely that at least one of the 2012 second fiddles would spend a lot of time in the media spotlight and consequently come to play an important role in the vote choice of the many valuable Independent voters in the next election.

Of course neither Hillary Clinton nor Marco Rubio ultimately played the part of second fiddle. Instead, incumbent Vice President Joe Biden returned to the bottom of the Democratic ticket, while Congressman Paul Ryan parterned with Romney on the Republican side. Though the impact that these men will have on voters in the 2012 election cannot be fully known at the time of this writing, media coverage patterns of these candidates offer some suggestive evidence. Biden's modest impact on the 2008 election, combined with the media's coverage of him during his first term in office suggest that he will likely affect few voters in the 2012 race. In contrast, the media attention received by Ryan since his introduction as a vice presidential candidate offers some hints that he might exhibit a stronger electoral impact, though it is unlikely he will match the impact of the Ferraro, Lieberman, Cheney (2004), or Palin candidacies.

Coming into the 2012 election as the incumbent, Joe Biden has been under the media's scrutiny for the past four years. As the analysis presented in Chapter 4 suggests, the nature of that coverage is likely a good predictor of the impact he will make on voters in the 2012 race. Incumbent VP candidates who receive more negative media coverage during their first terms tend to more greatly influence voter decision making at the time of their reelection. To investigate the media coverage Biden received in his first term in office, I replicated the content analysis conducted in earlier chapters by coding 25% of all the *New York Times* stories referencing Joe Biden between inauguration day in 2009 and Labor Day in 2012. While Biden's media coverage over this period was less positive than his 2008 election coverage, he still received solidly neutral ratings. Over the course of his first four years in office, about

93% of the stories referencing Biden took on a neutral tone and 81% portrayed a neutral image of him. The remainder of the stories leaned slightly negative – almost 5% of the stories took a negative tone and nearly 8% painted a negative image while only about 2% took a positive tone and 6.5% painted a postive image.

Early in his term, the media suggested that he would play a minor role as vice president. It was said that he had "the title, the residence and the security detail, but the position [had] been dummied down." (Stanley 2009), and was compared to a marginalized talk-show sidekick. "Mostly, President Obama treats him like a latter-day Paul Shaffer, humoring him briefly, then shunting him off-stage before he goes on too long" (Stanley 2009). As the years wore on, however, his involvement "in a wide array of projects and responsibilities with in the Obama administration" (NewYorkTimes.com 2009) gained note. The media often reported on his role as a key Congressional liasion and negotiator on domestic issues (Herszenhorrn and Lorber 2010; Hulse, Zeleny, and Steinhauer 2011; Landler 2010), as well as his inovlvement in key foreign policy decisions (Fahim and Kirkpatrick. 2011; Kershner 2010; Landler and Cooper 2010; Landler and Cooper 2011). By his third year in office, the media portrayed Biden as a trusted adviser to President Obama, calling him "the president's chief troubleshooter" and often mentioning that he is "always the last person in the room with the president" (Landler 2011). Findings from Chapter 6 suggest that voters pay attention to the political experience of vice presidential candidates, especially when they feel the veep is unprepared to assume the role of commander in chief if called upon. Given the media's portrayal of Biden as a competent and experienced partner to the president, voters likely have little reason for concern on this count, and thus their impressions of his experience will likely play little role in their vote choice.

The media presents an equally mixed portrait of Biden's personal image. Stories tend to focus on his "famously garrulous" style (Sanger 2009) which often leads to humorous and embarrasing gaffes, but also on his amiable personality and ability to connect to the common man. Calling him "uber-exuberant," "gaffe prone," and suggesting he suffers from "foot-in-mouth syndrome" (Dowd 2010), the media readily reported Biden's verbal misteps over his four years in office. From calling the president's special representative for Afghanistan and Pakistan "the most egostistical bastard I've ever met" (Baker 2010) to taking a public stand on same-sex marriage before the president (Baker and Sussman 2012), Biden gained "a reputation for speaking voluably, and sometimes going beyond official policy" (Kramer 2009). Alongside coverage of such "Joe Bombs," as some on his 2008 campaign staff called Biden's "verbal misadventures" (Leibovich 2012c), the media also presented a picture of Biden as an "unyielding optimist" whose "passionate and upbeat" personality makes voters "light up" (Stolberg 2010). Calling him "Regular Joe Biden" (Leibovich 2012b) and "Amtrak Joe" (Isaacson 2009) the media suggests to voters that he is a "carefree guy, someone [they] could relate to" (Leibovich 2012a). Given the mixed image the media has offered voters, it is unlikely most will have formed impressions of him strong enough to impact their vote come November.

In the 2008 presidential election Joe Biden influenced the votes of about 15% of Independent voters, an impact slightly below that of the typical Democratic vice presidential candidate since 1972. Media coverage of his first term in office suggests his impact in 2012 will likely be similarly marginal. In the 2008 election period, Biden scored a 2.14 (out of 3) on the the media tone variable. During his first term in office, he averaged a similarly neutral media tone score of 1.97. His media image scores were comparable, with a 2008 campaign period score of 2.12 and an incumbency period score of 1.99. As the results presented in Tables 4.3 and 4.4 suggest, previous incumbent vice presidential candidates with tone and image scores of similar mangnitude have impacted between 5.6% and 7.5% of Independent voters at reelection time. Consequently, it seems likely that Biden's influence in the 2012 election will be equally muted.

While voters have had four years of media coverage by which to judge Joe Biden, they will only be able to rely on a campaign season's worth of media attention focused on Paul Ryan. To get an idea of what such coverage might look like, I replicated the analyses condcted in earlier chapters by coding 50% of all *New York Times* stories referencing Paul Ryan between August 11th (the day on which Romney introduced Ryan as his vice presidential choice) and Labor Day, 2012.[8] Overall, this early media coverage of Ryan strikes a remarkably neutral tone. Over the short period examined here, about 89% of the stories referencing Ryan took on a neutral tone and 85% portrayed a neutral image of him. The remainder of the stories leaned negative – 8.5% of the stories took a negative tone and nearly 10% painted a negative image while almost 3% took a positive tone and almost 6% painted a postive image.

As we might expect, the media has spent a good deal of time discussing Ryan's political experience and qualifications for the VP job. While generally reporting neutrally about his experience in Congress, the media offers a somewhat mixed assessment of his ability to handle the responsibilities of the vice presidency. While three-quarters of the coverage mentioning his experience simply reports that he served in Congress, the remainder of the coverage is equally critical and complimentary. Viewing Ryan as "the good think-tanker-as-politician" (Lowery 2012) who can have "in-depth and substantive" (Barbaro 2012) conversations about domestic policy, the media paint Ryan as an intelligent and informed candidate. Drawing particular attention to his work as the chairman of the House Budget Committee (Cooper 2012; Goodnough 2012; Hulse 2012) and his policy positions regarding Medicare (Brooks and Collins 2012; Dowd 2012; Goodnough 2012), the media present Ryan as "the wonk prince of the Republican Party" (Bruni 2012). Suggesting that "it won't be another Palin moment" (Peters 2012) when campaign rhetoric turns to substantive issues, the media report that Ryan "easily passed the 'deer in the headlights' test that undermined" previous Republican presidential nominees (Gabriel 2012a). At the same time, Ryan's foreign policy experience has been questioned. Noting Ryan's lack of experience in this area, especially in comparison to his Democratic counterpart, some wondered if Ryan might be put "on the spot" during the vice presidential debates (Gabriel 2012a). Others report on Ryan's frequent foreign policy briefings (Gabriel 2012b) and his often quoted defense that he has "a lot more experience than Barack Obama did when he became president" (Strauss 2012), suggesting that there was concern on this point.

The analyses presented in Chapter 6 suggest that when the media negatively portrays a vice presidential candidate's political experience, the candidate is likely to impact more voters. Given the mixed coverage of Ryan's political experience to date, it is possible that voters might be affected by his candidacy. Should the media focus predominantly on Ryan's thin foreign policy experience, voters are likely to consider their feelings about him when casting a ballot. Conversely, should the media focus more on domestic issues where Ryan has much more experience, the public will likely be less influenced by their impressions of him. Since 72% of potential voters named the economy as the nation's most important problem in a September, 2012, poll (Gallup Poll 2012) it seems unlikely that the media negativity surrounding Ryan's limited foreign policy experience will lead to his candidacy exhibiting a very strong electoral impact.

Thus, it appears that voter sentiment about neither Ryan nor Biden is likely to greatly impact the outcome of the 2012 election. Still, there are some signs that their candidacies will impact the contours of the campaign season. Since the media portrays both veep candidates as intelligent, competent policy experts who have an ability to speak in detail about issues in the spotlight, voters are more likely to be treated to a "real debate" (Friedman 2012; Krugman 2012) on substantive issues than in previous campaigns. In fact, the media has been much more likely to mention issues in their coverage of both Biden and Ryan than they have been in their coverage of other vice presidential candidates. While only about 39% of the coverage of vice presidential candidates since 1972 has contained references to substantive issues, more than half (53.4%) of the coverage of Biden's first term in office and about 87% of the early coverage of Ryan has mentioned at least one substantive issue. So while the part that these second fiddles play may mean little to the eventual outcome of the election, their presence may change the song voters hear over the course of the campaign.

Notes

[1] Ferraro's impact score is 3.04 standard deviations above the mean vice presidential impact score, and Palin's media volume score is 3.23 standard deviations above the mean volume of coverage for vice presidential candidates.

[2] Feelings about the typical Democratic vice presidential candidate affect about 2.1% of the entire electorate while feelings about the typical Republican vice presidential candidate sway about 1.4% of the electorate's votes.

[3] The typical Democratic presidential candidate influenced about 5% of the electorate while the typical Republican candidate swayed about 3.5%.

[4] The popular vote margin in the 2000 election was 0.51%; the margin in 1976 was 2.06%; and the margin in 2004 was 2.46%.

[5] A vice presidential candidate exerting as much impact as Geraldine Ferraro (i.e., one influencing about 5.3% of the electorate) could have affected the outcome of two additional elections. Such a candidate might have affected the 1992 and 2004 elections, which were decided by 202 and 35 electoral votes, respectively. A vice presidential candidate exhibiting Ferraro's impact would have affected a predicted 208 electoral votes in the 1992 and 141 electoral votes in 2004, thus changing the election outcomes.

[6] The unstandardized regression coefficients for Democratic and Republican vice presidential candidates over the 1972-2008 period correlates at -0.589 (p=0.08, two-tailed), and the percent of Independent voters affected correlates at -0.416 (p=0.232).

[7] The percentage of media garnered by these nominees correlates at -0.398 (p=0.03) and the relative media coverage of these nominees correlates at -0.298 (p=0.04).

[8] Because relatively few stories had been published in this period, I chose to code 50% of the stories instead of 25% as in previous analyses. In total, 71 stories were coded for this analysis.

Appendix A:
Survey Measures and Coding

Following are the variables and coding scheme used in the regression analyses. All variables are from the National Election Studies Cumulative Dataset. Available online at: http://www.electionstudies.org/studypages/download/datacenter_all.htm

Vote Choice:
1=vote for Democratic presidential ticket; 0=vote for Republican presidential ticket (a vote for any other candidate is coded as missing and excluded from analysis)

> How about the election for President? Did you vote for a candidate for President? (IF YES:) Who did you vote for?

Presidential and Vice-Presidential Candidate Ratings:
Ratings ranging from 0 (coldest) to 100 (warmest) for each presidential and vice presidential candidate in each election year.

> I'd like to get your feelings toward some of our political leaders and other people who are in the news these days. I'll read the name of a person and I'd like you to rate that person using something we call the feeling thermometer. Ratings between 50 and 100 degrees mean that you feel favorably and warm toward the person; ratings between 0 and 50 degrees mean that you don't feel favorably toward the person and that you don't care too much for that person. You would rate the person at the 50 degree mark if you don't feel particularly warm or cold toward the person. If we come to a person whose name you don't recognize, you don't need to rate that person. Just tell me and we'll move on to the next one. If you do recognize the name, but you don't feel particularly warm or cold toward the person, then you would rate the person at the 50 degree mark. (pre-election rating)

Economic Evaluations:
Respondent evaluation of his/her personal/family economic situation over the past year: 1=gotten worse; 2=stayed about the same; 3=gotten better.

> We are interested in how people are getting along financially these days. Would you say that you are better off or worse off financially than you were a year ago. Would you say that you are better off, worse off, or just about the same financially as you were a year ago?

Female:
Sex of respondent: 1=female; 0=male.

Age:
Respondent's age.

> Age in years, from this question: What is the month, day and year of your birth?

Minority:
Respondent race/ethnicity: 1=non-white; 0=white.

> In addition to being American, what do you consider your main ethnic group or nationality group? White, Black, Asian, Native American, Hispanic, Other.

Education:
Respondent's formal education level.

> 1=Grade school or less (0-8 grades); 2=high school (12 grades or fewer); 3=some college (13 grades or more, but no degree); 4=College or advanced degree.

Democrat:
Dichotomous variable indicating whether respondent self-identifies as a Democrat (1) or not (0). Those leaning toward the Democratic party are included as Democratic adherents.

Republican:
Dichotomous variable indicating whether respondent self-identifies as a Republican (1) or not (0). Those leaning toward the Republican party are included as Republican adherents.

> Generally speaking, do you usually think of yourself as a Republican, a Democrat, an Independent, or what? (IF INDEPENDENT, OTHER OR NO PREFERENCE]) Do you think of yourself as closer to the Republican or Democratic party?

Liberal:
Dichotomous variable indicating whether respondent self-identifies as extremely liberal, liberal or slightly liberal (1) or not (0).

Conservative:
Dichotomous variable indicating whether respondent self-identifies as extremely conservative, conservative or slightly conservative (1) or not (0).

> We hear a lot of talk these days about liberals and conservatives. Here is a 7-point scale on which the political views that people might hold are arranged from extremely liberal to extremely conservative. Where would you place yourself on this scale, or haven't you thought much about this?

Appendix B:
Selection and Coding
of Media Content

For the present study, a stratified random sample of stories about candidates in presidential general elections between 1972 and 2008 was taken. The sample was stratified on candidate-year so that 25% of the stories about each candidate in each year were selected and coded for content. While there is, unfortunately, "no universally accepted set of criteria for selecting the size of a sample" (Neuendorf 2002: 88), some studies have suggested that properly drawn random samples as small as twelve or fourteen adequately represent the population in general (see e.g., Lacy, Robinson, and Riffe 1995; Stempel 1952), and some even argue that a carefully drawn sample of six days can be effective in representing one year of content of the *New York Times* online (Wang and Riffe 2010). At the same time, others who recommend calculating the desired sample size based on the desired confidence level and using standard errors and confidence intervals to arrive at the appropriate sample size (Neuendorf 2002: 89), demonstrate that about 2,400 cases would result in a confidence interval of +/- 2% points (at the 95% confidence level). Of the 37,222 stories referencing all major party candidates in presidential elections between 1972 and 2008, a total of 9,306 were coded for content. A sample of this size results in a confidence interval of less than +/-1% (at the 95% confidence level).

Story Selection

For each candidate in each election year, a random sample of 25% of all stories published between Labor Day and Election Day mentioning the candidate were selected. To ensure a truly random sample, I first assigned a unique code to each story by numbering the stories in consecutive order. For example, the 808 stories referencing Sarah Palin were numbered 1 through 808. I next calculated the number of articles that constituted 25% of the total articles for each candidate. For example, 25% (202) of the 808 Palin stories were selected for content analysis. To randomly select 25% of the stories related to each candidate for coding, I used an online random number generator (http://www.random.org/integer-sets/) to select the specific stories for coding. For example, in the Palin case, I generated 202 random numbers between 1 and 808 and retrieved the stories with those codes from the LexisNexis Academic database. Since the random number generator returned the numbers: 3, 7, 9, 14, etc. for the Palin search, I downloaded the third, seventh, ninth, fourteenth, etc. stories from the list of stories referencing Palin for content coding. This procedure was repeated for each candidate in each year.

Coding Reliability

A graduate research assistant, serving as the primary coder, then read each of the randomly selected articles and coded its content using the coding scheme presented in Table B.1 below.[1] Since the value of these measures depends on the quality of the coding (Kolbe and Burnett 1991: 248; Neuendorf 2002: 141; Singletary 1993: 294; Tinsley and Weiss 2000: 98), I conducted a series of reliability tests to ensure that this coder accurately and consistently analyzed the content of the news stories.

While there is no set standard for how large a subsample should be utilized in such reliability analyses, the general consensus is that "the reliability sub-sample should probably never be smaller than 50 and should rarely need to be larger than about 300" (Neuendorf, 2002: 159; see also Potter and Levin-Donnerstein 1999; Wimmer and Dominick 1991). For each candidate in each year, a second, independent coder read and coded a 5% random sample of the stories for each candidate in each year originally read and coded by the primary coder.[2] I then conducted a series of inter-coder reliability tests that compared the first coder's ratings of the stories to those of second coder.

Though Popping (1988) identified more than 40 different ways to measure intercoder reliability, "there are few standards or guidelines available concerning how to properly calculate and report intercoder reliability" (Lombard, Snyder-Duch, and Bracken 2002: 588). Simple percent agreement – that is, "the percentage of all coding decisions made by pairs of coders on which the coders agree" (Lombard, Snyder-Duch, and Bracken 2002: 590) – remains a commonly used metric. While this measure of reliability has the advantage of being simple, intuitive, and easy to calculate, it fails to account for times when the coders will agree by chance. Thus, the percentage agreement measure will likely be a liberal measure of reliability that over-estimates inter-coder agreement (Lombard, Snyder-Duch, and Bracken 2002; Perrault and Leigh 1989; Seun and Lee 1985). And, unfortunately, corrections to this measure tend to over-correct for the problem and lead to under-estimates of agreement (Lombard, Snyder-Duch, and Bracken 2002).

Table B.1: Coding Scheme

Identifying Information	
Story ID	unique identification code for each story
Date of Story	in MM.DD.YY format
Section	section of newspaper in which story appears
Page	page on which story begins
Story Length	number of words in story
Candidate Covered	1=McGovern72; 2=Shriver72; 3=Nixon72; 4=Agnew72; 5=Carter76; 6=Mondale76; 7=Ford76; 8=Dole76; 9=Carter80; 10=Mondale80; 11=Reagan80; 12=Bush80 ; 13=Mondale84; 14=Ferrarro84; 15=Reagan84; 16=Bush84; 17=Dukakis88; 18=Bentsen88; 19=Bush88; 20=Quayle88; 21=Clinton92; 22=Gore92; 23=Bush92; 24=Quayle92; 25=Clinton96; 26=Gore96; 27=Dole96; 28=Kemp96; 29=Gore00; 30=Lieberman00; 31=Bush00; 32=Cheney00; 33=Kerry04; 34=Edwards04; 35=Bush04; 36=Cheney04; 37=Obama08; 38=Biden08; 39=McCain08; 40=Palin08
Content of Coverage	
Intensity of Coverage	The amount of coverage of the candidate in the story: *3 = A lot; 2 = Medium amount; 1 = Very Little*
Overall Tone	In your opinion, what is the *overall* tone of the story with regard to this candidate? *0=No Overall Tone; 1=Negative Tone; 2=Neutral/Balanced Tone; 3=Positive Tone*
Candidate Image	Imagine you are in charge of this person's campaign. How satisfied are you with your candidate's image/description in this story? *0=no image/description of candidate; 1=Unsatisfied; 2=Neutral; 3=Satisfied*
Candidate Characteristics and Traits	
How does the article mention and/or assess the candidate's . . .	
Race	race/ethnicity?
Sex	gender?
Religion	religious preference/practice?
Marital Status	marital status?
0=no mention at all; 1=neutral or balanced mention/assessment; 2=negative mention/assessment; 3=positive mention/assessment; 4=don't know	
How does the article mention and/or assess these candidate traits . . .	
Honesty	Honesty
Morality	Morality/Decency
Intelligence	Intelligence/Knowledgeable
Compassion	Compassionate/Empathetic/Cares about people
Inspiration	Inspiring
Leadership	Strong leader
Experience	level of political experience mentioned/assesses?
0=no mention at all; 1=neutral or balanced mention/assessment; 2=negative mention/assessment; 3=positive mention/assessment; 4=don't know	

As an alternative to these measures, Krippendorff's (2004) alpha represents a "well regarded and very flexible" (Lombard, Snyder-Duch, and Bracken 2010) measure of intercoder reliability. The measure can be used with any number of coders, it accounts for chance agreements, and it is explicitly designed to be used with variables measured at different levels of measurement from nominal to ratio (a point which is especially important given the nature of the variables in the current study). Like the percentage agreement measure, Krippendorff's alpha ranges from 0 to 1, with zero indicating no intercoder agreement on the coding of variable and 1 representing perfect agreement on the coding of the variable.

Table B.2 reports both the percent agreement and Krippendorff's alpha for each variable. The values reported in this table are for the entire sample of stories. As this table suggests, the levels of intercoder reliability are quite high. The coders agreed on the coding of variables between 83% and 100% of the time, with Krippendorff's alpha values ranging between 0.76 and 1.00. Not surprisingly, measures related to the more objective references to candidates' characteristics, particularly race, sex, religious preference, and marital status, exhibit the highest levels of reliability. At the same time, the more subjective measures related to tone of coverage or candidate image exhibit lower, yet respectable, levels of agreement.

Table B.2: Reliability Analysis

Variable	Percent Agreement	Krippendorff's Alpha
Content of Coverage		
Intensity of Coverage	0.84	0.77
Overall Tone	0.85	0.78
Candidate Image	0.83	0.76
Candidate Characteristics		
Appearance	0.97	0.91
Race	1.00	1.00
Sex	1.00	1.00
Religion	1.00	1.00
Marital Status	1.00	1.00
Candidate Traits		
Character	0.96	0.88
Honesty	0.95	0.90
Morality	0.94	0.81
Intelligence	0.96	0.84
Compassion	0.93	0.79
Inspiration	0.92	0.80
Leadership	0.96	0.93
Experience	0.99	0.97

Notes

¹ Following established practice (Kaid and Wadsworth 1989, Lacy and Riffe 1996, Wimmer and Dominick 1991), the coding scheme presented here was piloted test using a subset of 5% of the total randomly selected stories (465 stories). Two independent coders read and coded these 465 stories according to an earlier draft of the coding scheme. Following the completion of the pilot test coding, inter-coder reliability checks similar to those presented here were performed and the coding instrument was revised to minimize coding discrepancies.

² A minimum of 50 cases for each candidate-year were included in the reliability analyses. Thus, when a candidate was mentioned in less than 1,000 stories in a given year, more than 5% of the news stories for that year were included in the reliability analysis.

Bibliography

ABC News. 2000. "Early Criticism of Clinton Wins Praise for Lieberman." *ABC News Good Morning America Poll* August 8. Accessed January 4, 2012: http://abcnews.go.com/images/pdf/824a1Lieberman.pdf

ABC News. 2009. "Full Transcript: Charlie Gibson Interviews GOP Vice Presidential Candidate Sarah Palin." November 23. Accessed September 3, 2012: http://abcnews.go.com/Politics/Vote2008/full-transcript-gibson-interviews-sarah-palin/story?id=9159105&singlePage=true#.UET0-NZlTn0

ABC News. 2012. "Chris Christie Illustrates Worth of VP Role with Biden Joke." August 6. Accessed September 3, 2012: http://abcnews.go.com/blogs/politics/2012/08/chris-christie-illustrates-worth-of-vp-role-withbiden-joke/

Adkison, Danny M. 1982. "The Electoral Significance of the Vice Presidency." *Presidential Studies Quarterly* 12: 330-336.

Allsop, Dee and Herbert F. Weisberg. 1988. "Measuring Change in Party Identification in an Election Campaign." *American Journal of Political Science* 32: 996-1017.

Althaus, Scott L., Peter F. Nardulli, and Daron R. Shaw. 2002. "Candidate Appearances in Presidential Elections, 1972–2000." *Political Communication* 19: 49-72.

Ansolabehere, Stephen, Shanto Iyengar, and Adam Simon. 1999. "Replicating Experiments Using Aggregate and Survey Data: The Case of Negative Advertising and Turnout." *American Political Science Review* 93: 901-910.

Ansolabehere, Stephen, Shanto Iyengar, Adam Simon, and Nicholas Valentino. 1994. "Does Attack Advertising Demobilize the Electorate?" *American Political Science Review* 88: 829-838.

Ansolabehere, Stephen and Shanto Iyengar. 1995. *Going Negative*. New York: Free Press.

Apple, R.W., Jr. 1991. "Though Quayle Seems Shoo-In for '92, Leading the '96 Ticket Is No Sure Bet." *The New York Times,* May 19.

Arceneaux, Kevin and David W. Nickerson. 2005. "Two Field Experiments Testing Negative Campaign Tactics." *Paper Presented at the Annual Meeting of the American Political Science Association.*

Avlon, John. 2012. "Could Pro-Choice Nevada Governor Brian Sandoval Be the GOP's Great Hope?" *The Daily Beast*, February 24.

Baker, Peter. 2010. "Book Says Afghanistan Divided White House." *The New York Times*, September 22.

Baker, Peter and Salia Sussman. 2012. "New Poll Finds Voters Dubious of Obama's Announcement on Same-Sex Marriage." *The New York Times*, May 15.

Barbaro, Michael. 2012. "The Courtship Before Romney Elevated Ryan." *The New York Times*, August 19.

Barker, David C. 1999. "Rushed Decisions." *Journal of Politics* 61: 527-39.

Barker, David C. 2002. *Rushed to Judgment*. New York: Columbia University Press.

Bartels, Larry M. 1996. "Politicians and the Press: Who Leads, Who Follows?" Paper presented at the Annual Meeting of the American Political Science Association.

Bartels, Larry M. 2002. "Beyond the Running Tally: Partisan Bias in Political Perceptions." *Political Behavior* 24: 117-150.

Basil, Michael, Caroline Schooler, and Byron Reeves. 1991. "Positive and Negative Political Advertising: Effectiveness of Ads and Perceptions of Candidates." In Frank Biocca, ed. *Television and Political Advertising*, Vol. 1. Hillsdale, NJ: Lawrence Erlbaum, 245-62.

Baumgartner, Jody C. 2008. "The Veepstakes: Forecasting Vice Presidential Selection in 2008." *PS: Political Science and Politics* 41: 765-772

Bean, Clive. 1993. "The Electoral Influence of Party Leader Images in Australia and New Zealand." *Comparative Political Studies* 26: 111-32.

Berelson, Bernard R., Paul F. Lazarsfeld, and William N. McPhee. 1954. *Voting*. Chicago, IL: University of Chicago Press.

Berinsky, Adam J. and Tali Mendelberg. 2005. "The Indirect Effects of Discredited Stereotypes in Judgments of Jewish Leaders." *American Journal of Political Science* 49: 845-864.

Berke, Richard. 2000. "The 2000 Campaign: Conservative Organizaitons; Some Quiet Support on Polarizing Topics." *The New York Times*, September 27.

Blumenthal, Ralph. 1984. "Jury Investigating 2 Zaccaro Dealings." *The New York Times*, October 23.

Bobo, Lawrence and Frank Gilliam. 1990. "Race, Sociopolitical Participation, and Black Empowerment." *American Political Science Review* 84: 377-93.

Brady, Henry E. and Richard Johnston. 1987. "What's the Primary Message: Horse Race or Issue Journalism." In Gary R. Orren and Nelson W. Polsby, eds. *Media and Momentum: The New Hampshire Primary and Nomination Politics*, Chatham, N. J.: Press, 127-186.

Brady, Henry E., Richard Johnston, and John Sides. 2006. "The Study of Political Campaigns." In Henry E. Brady and Richard Johnston, eds. *Capturing Campaign Effects*. Ann Arbor, MI: University of Michigan Press, 1-26.

Brooks, David and Gail Collins. 2012. "Between the Acts." *The New York Times*, September 2.

Brown, Steven D., Ronald D. Lambert, Barry J. Kay, and James E. Curtis. 1988. "In the Eye of the Beholder: Leader Images in Canada." *Canadian Journal of Political Science* 21: 729-55.

Brox, Brian J. and Madison L. Cassells. 2009. "The Contemporary Effects of Vice Presidential Nominees: Sarah Palin and the 2008 Presidential Campaign." *Journal of Political Marketing* 8: 349-363.

Bruni, Frank. 2012. "The Bold to Mitt's Bland." *The New York Times*, August 14.

Bryce, James. 1893. *The American Commonwealth*, Vol. 2. New York: Macmillan.

Campbell, Angus, Gerald Gurin, and Warren E. Miller. 1954. *The Voter Decides*. Evanston, IL: Row Peterson.

Campbell, Angus, Philip E. Converse, Warren E. Miller, and Donald E. Stokes. 1960. *The American Voter*. Chicago, IL: The University of Chicago Press.

Campbell, James E. 1992. "Forecasting the Presidential Vote in the States." *American Journal of Political Science* 36: 386-407.

Campbell, James E. 2000. *The American Campaign: U.S. Presidential Campaigns and the National Vote*. College Station, TX: Texas A&M University Press.

Campbell, James E., Syed Ali, and Farida Jalazai. 2006. "Forecasting Presidential Vote in the States, 1948-2004: An Update, Revision, and Extension of a State-Level Presidential Forecasting Model." In Wayne P. Steger, Sean Q. Kelly, and J. Mark Wrighton, eds. *Campaigns and Political Marketing*. New York: The Haworth Press, 33-57.

Capuzzo, Jill P. 2008. "Scrutinizing Both Tickets, At the Top and the Bottom." *New York Times,* October 26.

Carlin, Diana B. and Kelly L. Winfrey. 2009. "Have You Come a Long Way, Baby? Hillary Clinton, Sarah Palin, and Sexism in 2008 Campaign Coverage. *Communication Studies* 60: 326-343.

Carsey, Thomas M. 2000. *Campaign Dynamics: The Race for Governor*. Ann Arbor, MI: University of Michigan Press.

CBS News. 2011. "60 Minutes/Vanity Fair Poll: July Edition." June 26. Accessed January 13, 2012: http://www.cbsnews.com/stories/2011/06/26/60minutes /main20071988.shtml

CBS News Poll. 2008. "Obama Holding Off McCain." August 6. Accessed March 20, 2008: http://www.cbsnews.com/htdocs/pdf/Jul08B-VP.pdf

Chait, Johnathon. 2010. "Did Palin Hurt McCain?" *The New Republic*, October 15.

Cherlin, Andrew J. 2011. "For GOP Candidates, Rules to Love." *Washington Post,* December 16.

Chicago Tribune. 1991. "A Heart Flutters, a Nation Shudders." May 7.

Chusid, Ron. 2008. "The Polls: Palin, PUMAs, and Independents." *Liberal Values,* October 21.

Civettini, Andrew J.W. and David P. Redlawsk. 2009. "Voters, Emotions, and Memory." *Political Psychology* 30: 125-151.

Clinton, Joshua D. and John S. Lapinski. 2004. "'Targeted' Advertising and Voter Turnout: An Experimental Study of the 2000 Presidential Election." *Journal of Politics* 66: 69-96.

Cohen, Jeffrey E. 2001a. "'The Polls': Popular Views of the Vice President: Vice President Approval." *Presidential Studies Quarterly* 31: 142-149.

Cohen, Jeffrey E. 2001b. "'The Polls': Popular Views of the Vice President and Vice Presidential Favorability." *Presidential Studies Quarterly* 31: 349-357.

Cohen, Jeffrey E. 2008. *The Presidency in the Era of 24-Hour News*. Princeton, NJ: Princeton University Press.

Comstock, George and Erica Scharrer. 2005. *The Psychology of Media and Politics*. Burlington, MA: Elsevier.

Coombs, Steven. 1981. "Editorial Endorsements and Electoral Outcomes." In Michael MacKuen and Steven Coombs, eds. *More than News*. Beverly Hills, CA: Sage Publications, 181-191.

Cooper, Michael 2008. "McCain's Age May Figure in Choice of Running Mate." *New York Times*, February 28.

Cooper, Michael. 2012. "Facts Take a Beating in Acceptance Speeches." *The New York Times*, August 31.

Craig, Stephen C., James G. Kane, and Jason Gainous. 2005. "Issue-Related Learning in a Gubernatorial Campaign: A Panel Study." *Political Communication* 22: 483-503.

Dalton, Russell J., Paul A. Beck, and Robert Huckfeldt. 1998. "Partisan Cues and the Media." *American Political Science Review* 92: 111-26.

Daniels, Mark. 2008. "Did Sarah Palin Lose the Election for McCain?" *The Moderate Voice*, November 6.

David, Paul. 1967. "The Vice Presidency: Its Institutional Evolution and Contemporary Status." *Journal of Politics* 29: 721-48.

Delli Carpini, Michael X. and Scott Keeter. 1996. *What Americans Know about Politics and Why It Matters*. New Haven, CT: Yale University Press

Dolan, Kathleen. 1998. "Voting for Women in 'The Year of the Woman.'" *American Journal of Political Science* 42: 272-293.

Dowd, Maureen. 1984. "Challenges to Ferraro Bring Strong Responses Among Women." *The New York Times*, September 6.

Dowd, Maureen. 2004. "White House of Horrors." *The New York Times*, October 28.

Dowd, Maureen. 2010. "Isn't it Ironic?" *The New York Times*, June 13.

Dowd, Maureen. 2012. "Cruel Conservatives Throw a Masquerade Ball." *The New York Times*, September 2.

Downs, Anthony. 1957. *An Economic Theory of Democracy*. New York: Harper and Row.

Draper, Robert. 2008. "The Making (and Remaking and Remaking) of the Candidate." *The New York Times,* October 26.

Druckman, James N. 2004. "Priming the Vote: Campaign Effects in a U.S. Senate Election." *Political Psychology* 25: 577-594.

Druckman, James N. and Justin W. Holmes. 2004. "Does Presidential Rhetoric Matter? Priming and Presidential Approval." *Presidential Studies Quarterly* 34: 755-778.

Druckman, James N., Lawrence R. Jacobs, and Eric Ostermeier. 2004. "Candidate Strategies to Prime Issues and Image." *The Journal of Politics* 66: 1180-1202.

Druckman, James N. and Michael Parkin. 2005. "The Impact of Media Bias: How Editorial Slant Affects Voters." *Journal of Politics* 67: 1030-1142.

Dudley, Robert L. and Ronald B. Rapoport. 1989. "Vice-Presidential Candidates and the Home State Advantage: Playing Second Banana at Home and on the Road." *American Journal of Political Science* 33: 537-540.

Dwyer, Devin. 2011. "Clint Eastwood as VP? George H.W. Bush Considered It." *ABC News*, October 14. Accessed January 22, 2012. http://abcnews.go.com/blogs/politics/2011/10/clint-eastwood-as-vp-george-h-w-bush-considered-it/

Elis, Roy, D. Sunshine Hillygus, and Norman Nie. 2010. "The Dynamics of Candidate Evaluations and Vote Choice in 2008: Looking to the Past or the Future?" *Electoral Studies* 29: 582-593.

Erikson, Robert. 1976. "The Influence of Newspaper Endorsements in Presidential Elections." *American Journal of Political Science* 20: 207-34.

Fahim, Kareem and David D. Kirkpatrick. 2011. "Labor Actions Across Egypt Lend Momentum to Anti-Mubarak Protests." *The New York Times*, February 10.

Fair, Ray. 2009. "Presidential and Congressional Vote Share Equations." *American Journal of Political Science* 53: 55-72.

Fairbanks, Amanda M. 2008. "Young, Republican and Inspired by Palin." *New York Times,* October 29.

Fazio, Russell H., Joni R. Jackson, Bridget C. Dunton, and Carol J. Williams. 1995. "Variability in Automatic Activation as an Unobtrusive Measure of Racial Attitudes: A Bona Fide Pipeline?" *Journal of Personality and Social Psychology* 69: 1013-1027.

Fenno, Jr., Richard F. 1978. *Home Style: House Members In Their Districts.* Boston, MA: Little Brown.

Finkel, Steven E. and John Geer. 1998. "A Spot Check: Casting Doubt on the Demobilizing Effect of Attack Advertising." *American Journal of Political Science* 42: 573-95.

Finkel, Steven. 1993. "Reexamining the 'Minimal Effects' Model in Recent Presidential Elections." *Journal of Politics* 55:1-21.

Fiske, Susan T. 1980. "Attention and Weight in Person Perception: The Impact of Negative and Extreme Behavior." *Journal of Personality and Social Psychology* 61: 889-906.

Fiske, Susan T. and Shelley E. Taylor. 1991. *Social Cognition*, 2nd ed. New York: McGraw- Hill.

Fox, Richard L. and R.A.N. Smith. 1998. "The Role of Candidate Sex in Voter Decision-Making." *Political Psychology* 19: 405-419.

Franklin, Charles H. 1991. "Eschewing Obfuscation? Campaigns and the Perception of U.S. Senate Incumbents." *American Political Science Review* 85: 1193-2114.

Frankovic, Kathleen A. 1984. "The 1984 Election: The Irrelevance of the Campaign." *PS: Political Science and Politics* 18: 39-47.

Freedman, Paul and Kenneth M. Goldstein. 1999. "Measuring Media Exposure and the Effects of Negative Campaign Ads." *American Journal of Political Science* 43: 1189-1208.

Fridkin, Kim Leslie, and Patrick J. Kenney. 2004. "Do Negative Messages Work? The Impact of Negativity on Citizens' Evaluations of Candidates." *American Politics Research* 32: 570-605.

Friedman, Thomas L. 2012. "We Need a 'Conservative' Party." *The New York Times*, August 22.

Funk, Carolyn L. 1996. "Implications of Political Expertise in Candidate Trait Evaluations." *Political Research Quarterly* 50: 675-697.

Funk, Carolyn L. 1999. "Bringing the Candidate into Models of Candidate Evaluation." *The Journal of Politics* 61: 700-20.

Gabel, Matthew and Kenneth Scheve. 2007. "Estimating the Effect of Elite Communications on Public Opinion Using Instrumental Variables." *American Journal of Political Science* 51: 1013-28.

Gabriel, Trip. 2012a. "Ryan, Appearing at East in First Week on Trail, Begins to Look Ahead." *The New York Times*, August 18.

Gabriel, Trip. 2012b. "Ryan Dips into Foreign Affairs." *The New York Times*, August 20.

Gailey, Phil. 1984. "Bush-Ferraro Debate Today Seen as Altering Campaign Dynamics." *The New York Times*, October 11.

Gallup Poll. 2000. "Positive Public Reaction to Gore's Choice of Lieberman as VP." *Gallup Poll*, August 8. Accessed January 4, 2012: http://www.gallup.com/poll/2656/positive-public-reaction-gores-choice-lieberman.aspx

Gallup Poll. 2008. "Republicans' Enthusiasm Jumps After Convention." *Gallup Poll*, September 8. Accessed June 25, 2012: http://www.gallup.com/poll/110107/Republicans-Enthusiasm-Jumps-After-Convention.aspx

Gallup Poll. 2012. "Most Important Problem." *GallupPoll.com*, September 17. Accessed September 17, 2012: http://www.gallup.com/poll/1675/most-important-problem.aspx

Garand, James C. 1988. "Localism and Regionalism in Presidential Elections: Is There a Home State or Regional Advantage?" *Political Research Quarterly* 41: 85-103.

Gargan, Edward A. 1984. "In Buffalo, State of Economy is Key Campaign Issue." *New York Times*, October 24.

Gawronski, Bertram, and Galen Bodenhausen. 2006. "Associative and Propositional Processes in Evaluation: An Integrative Review of Implicit and Explicit Attitude Change." *Psychological Bulletin* 132: 692–731.

Gay, Claudine. 2001. "The Effect of Black Congressional Representation on Political Participation." *American Political Science Review* 95: 589-602.

Geer, John G. 2006. In Defense of Negativity: Attack Ads in Presidential Campaigns. Chicago, IL: University of Chicago Press.

Gelman, Andrew and Gary King. 1993. "Why Are American Presidential Elections Campaign Polls So Variable When Votes Are So Predictable?" *British Journal of Political Science* 23: 409-51.

Gilliam, Frank. 1996. "Exploring Minority Empowerment: Symbolic Politics, Governing Coalitions, and Traces of Political Style in Los Angeles." *American Journal of Political Science* 40: 56-81.

Goldstein, Joel K. 1982. The Modern American Vice Presidency: The Transformation of a Political Institution. Princeton, NJ: Princeton University Press.

Goldstein, Ken and Paul Freedman. 2002a. "Campaign Advertising and Voter Turnout: New Evidence for a Stimulation Effect." *Journal of Politics* 64: 721-740.

Goodnough, Abby. 2012. "2 Campaigns Differ Sharply on Medicaid, Seeking Vast Growth or Vast Cuts." *The New York Times*, September 1.

Graber, Doris A. 1984. Processing the News: How People Tame the Information Tide. New York: Longman.

Graham, Donald. 1974. "The Vice Presidency: From Cigar Store Indian to Crown Prince." *Washington Monthly* 6: 41.

Grossman, Michael Baruch and Martha Joynt Kumar. 1981. *Portraying the President: The White House and the News Media.* Baltimore, MD: Johns Hopkins University Press.

Guerriero, John. 2008. "Palin Picked." *Erie Times-News*, August 30.

Gurin, Patricia, Shirley Hatchett, and James S. Jackson. 1989. *Hope and Independence: Blacks' Response to Electoral and Party Politics*. New York: Russell Sage Foundation.

Hamilton, David L. and Mark P. Zanna. 1974. "Context Effects in Impression Formation: Changes in Connotative Meaning." *Journal of Personality and Social Psychology* 29: 649-654.

Hanlin, David. 1991. "Competent Quayle Unfairly Targeted." *The Cavalier Daily,* October 7.

Hayes, Danny. 2005. "Candidate Qualities Through a Partisan Lens: A Theory of Trait Ownership." *American Journal of Political Science* 49: 908-923.

Hayes, Danny. 2009. "Has Television Personalized Voting Behavior?" *Political Behavior* 31: 231-260.

Herbert, Bob. 2008a. "A Choice and An Echo." *The New York Times,* October 28.

Herbert, Bob. 2008b. "She's Not Ready." *New York Times,* September 12.

Herr, J. Paul. 2002. "The Impact of Campaign Appearances in the 1996 Election.*" Journal of Politics* 64: 904-913.

Herszenhorrn, David M. and Janie Lorber. 2010. "Democrats Yield as Senate Passes Big Tax Package." *The New York Times*, December 16.

Hetherington, Marc J. 1996. "The Media's Role in Forming Voters' National Economic Evaluations in 1992." *American Journal of Political Science* 40: 372-395.

Hill, Jeffrey S., Elaine Rodriquez, and Amanda E. Wooden. 2010. "Stump Speeches and Road Trips: The Impact of State Campaign Appearances in Presidential Elections." *PS: Political Science and Politics* 43: 243-254.

Hiller, Mark and Douglas Kriner. 2008. "Institutional Change and the Dynamics of Vice Presidential Selection." *Presidential Studies Quarterly* 38: 401-421.

Hillygus, D. Sunshine and Todd G. Shields. 2008. *The Persuadable Voters: Wedge Issues in Presidential Campaigns.* Princeton, NJ: Princeton University Press.

Hillygus, D. Sunshine. 2005. "The Dynamics of Turnout Intention in Election 2000." *Journal of Politics* 67: 50-68.

Holbrook, Thomas M, and Scott D. McClurg. 2005. "The Mobilization of Core Supporters: Campaigns, Turnout, and Electoral Composition in United States Presidential Elections." *American Journal of Political Science* 49: 689-703.

Holbrook, Thomas M. 1991. "Presidential Elections in Time and Space." *American Journal of Political Science* 35: 91-109.

Holbrook, Thomas M. 1994. "Campaigns, National Conditions, and U.S. Presidential Elections." *American Journal of Political Science* 38: 973-98.

Holbrook, Thomas M. 1996. *Do Campaigns Matter?* Thousand Oaks, CA: Sage Publications, Inc.

Holian, David B. 2004. "He's Stealing My Issues! Clinton's Crime Rhetoric and the Dynamics of Issue Ownership." *Political Behavior* 26: 95-124.

Huber, Gregory A. and Kevin Arceneaux. 2007. "Identifying the Persuasive Effects of Presidential Advertising." *American Journal of Political Science* 51: 957-77.

Huddy, Leonie and Nayda Terkildsen. 1993. "Gender Stereotypes and the Perception of Male and Female Candidates." *American Journal of Political Science* 37: 119-147.

Hulse, Carl, Jeff Zeleny, and Jennifer Steinhauer. 2011. "House Passes Deal to Raise Debt Cap and Defuse Crisis." *The New York Times,* August 2.

Hulse, Carl. 2012. "Ryan to Reassure Middle Class and Renew Attack on 'Obamacare.'" *The New York Times*, August 30.

Hurwitz, Jay A. 1980. "Presidential Eligibility and Selection Patterns." *Polity* 12: 509-521.

Institute for Social Research. 2010. "Two U-M ISR Studies Named to NSF 'Sensational 60' List." *University of Michigan.* May 28. Accessed January 4, 2012: http://www.isr.umich.edu/home/news/nsf-sensational.html

Isaacson, Andy. 2009. "Riding the Rails." *The New York Times*, March 8.

Iyengar, Shanto, and Donald Kinder. 1987. *News that Matters.* Chicago, IL: Chicago University Press.

Jacobs, Lawrence and Robert Shapiro. 1994. "Issues, Candidate Image, and Priming: The Use of Private Polls in Kennedy's 1960 Presidential Campaign." *American Political Science Review*, 88: 527-540.

Jamieson, Kathleen H. 1995. *Beyond the Double Bind: Women and Leadership.* New York: Oxford University Press.

Johnson-Cartee, Karen S. and Gary Copeland. 1989. "Southern Voters' Reaction to Negative Political Ads in the 1986 Election." *Journalism Quarterly* 66: 188-193.

Johnston, Richard and Emily Thorson. 2009. "Sarah Palin's Approval Ratings Moved John McCain's Support with Unparalleled Precision." *Boston Review,* September/October. Accessed February 7, 2012: http://bostonreview.net/BR34.5/johnston_thorson.php

Johnston, Richard, Michael Gray Hagen, and Kathleen Hall Jamieson. 2004. *The 2000 Presidential Election and the Foundations of Party Politics.* New York: Cambridge University Press.

Kahn, Kim Fridkin and Patrick J. Kenney. 2000. "How Negative Campaigning Enhances Knowledge of Senate Elections." In James A. Thurber, Candice J. Nelson, and David A. Dulio, eds. *Crowded Airwaves: Campaign Advertising in Elections.* Washington, D.C.: Brookings Institution, 65-95.

Kahn, Kim Fridkin, and Patrick J. Kenney. 2002. "The Slant of the News." *American Political Science Review* 96: 381-94.

Kahn, Kim Fridkin. 1994. "Does Gender Make a Difference? An Experimental Examination of Sex Stereotypes and Press Patterns in Statewide Campaigns." *American Journal of Political Science* 38:162-195.

Kahn, Kim Fridkin. 1996. The Political Consequences of Being a Woman: How Stereotypes Influence the Conduct and Consequences of Political Campaigns. New York: Columbia University Press.

Kahn, Kim, and Patrick J. Kenney. 2004. *No Holds Barred: Negativity in U.S. Senate Campaigns.* Upper Saddle River, NJ: Pearson Prentice Hall.

Kahneman, Daniel, Paul Slovic, and Amos Tversky, Eds. 1982. *Judgement Under Uncertainty: Heuristics and Biases.* New York: Cambridge.

Kaid, Lynda L., Sandra L. Myers, Val Pipps, and Jan Hunter. 1984. "Sex Role Perceptions and Televised Political Advertising: Comparing Male and Female Candidates." *Women and Politics* 4: 41-53.

Kaid, Lynda L. and Anne Johnston Wadsworth. 1989. "Content Analysis." In Philip Emmert and Larry L. Barker, eds. *Measurement of Communication Behavior*. New York: Longman, 197-217.

Karouse, David E. and L. Reid Hanson. 1972. "Negativity in Evaluations." In Edward E. Jones, David E. Kanouse, Harold H. Kelley, Richard E. Nisbett, Stuart Valins, and Bernard Weiner, eds. *Attribution: Perceiving Causes of Behavior*. Morriston, N.J.: General Learning Press, 47-62.

Kelleher, Christine A. and Jennifer Wolak. 2006. "Priming Presidential Approval: The Conditionality of Issue Effects." *Political Behavior* 28: 193-210.

Keller, Bill. 2012. "Just the Ticket." *New York Times*, January 8.

Kensinger, Elizabeth A. 2007. "Negative Emotion Enhances Memory Accuracy: Behavioral and Neuroimaging Evidence." *Current Directions in Psychological Science 16*: 213–218

Kenski, Kate. 2010. "The Palin Effect and Vote Preference in the 2008 Presidential Election." *American Behavioral Scientist* 54: 222-238.

Kershner, Isabel. 2010. "Israel Confirms New Building in East Jerusalem." *The New York Times*, March 25.

Kinder, Donald R. 1983. "Presidential Traits." *Report to the NES Board of Overseers*. Center for Political Studies, University of Michigan.

Kinder, Donald R. 1986. "Presidential Character Revisited." In Richard R. Lau and David O. Sears, eds. *Political Cognition: The 19th Annual Carnegie Symposium on Cognition*. Hillsdale, NJ: Lawrence Erlbaum Associates, 233-256.

Kinder, Donald R., Mark D. Peters, Robert P. Abelson, and Susan T. Fiske. 1980. "Presidential Prototypes." *Political Behavior* 2: 315-337.

Kinsley, Michael. 2008. "White Men in Suits." *New York Times*, November 4.

Klapper, Joseph. 1960. *The Effects of Mass Communication*. Glencoe, IL: The Free Press.

Kolbe, Richard H. and Melissa S. Burnett. 1991. "Content-Analysis Research: An Examination of Applications with Directives for Improving Research Reliability and Objectivity." *Journal of Consumer Research* 18: 243-250.

Kovaleski, Serge F. 2008. "Alaska Inquiry Concludes Palin Abused Powers." *The New York Times*, October 11.

Kramer, Andrew E. 2009. "New Biden Criticism Surprises Russia." *The New York Times*, July 26.

Krebs, Timothy B. 1998. "The Determinants of Candidates' Vote Share and the Advantages of Incumbency in City Council Elections." *American Journal of Political Science* 42: 921-935.

Krippendorff, Klaus. 2004. Content Analysis: An Introduction to its Methodology, 2nd ed. Thousand Oaks, CA: Sage.

Krosnick, Jon A. and Lautra A. Brannon. 1993. "The Impact of the Gulf War on the Ingredients of Presidential Evaluations: Multidimensional Effects of Political Involvement." *American Political Science Review* 87: 963-975.

Krosnick, Jon A. and Donald R. Kinder. 1990. "Altering the Foundations of Popular Support for the President Through Priming: Reagan and the Iran-Contra Affair." *American Political Science Review* 84: 495-512.

Krugman, Paul. 2004. "The Falling Scales." *The New York Times*, October 5.

Krugman, Paul. 2012. "An Unserious Man." *The New York Times*, August 20.

Lacy, Stephen, Kay Robinson, and Daniel Riffe. 1995. "Sample Size in Content Analysis of Weekly Newspapers." *Journalism and Mass Communication Quarterly* 72: 336-345.

Landler, Mark. 2010. "Clinton's Role as a Lobbyist Expands." *The New York Times,* November 18.

Landler, Mark. 2011. "Obama's Growing Trust in Biden is Reflected in His Call on Troops." *The New York Times*, June 25.

Landler, Mark and Helene Cooper. 2010. "U.S. Fears Election Strife in Iraq Could Affect Pullout." *The New York Times*, March 4.

Landler, Mark and Helene Cooper. 2011. "Mideast Allies Favor Stability Over Immediate Change in Egypt, Diplomats Tell U.S." *The New York Times*, February 9.

Lang, Annie. 1991. "Emotion, Formal Features, and Memory for Televised Political Advertisements." In Frank Biocca, ed. *Television and Political Advertising*, Vol. 1. Hillsdale, NJ: Lawrence Erlbaum, 221-43.

Lau, Richard R. and Gerald M. Pomper. 2004. *Negative Campaigning: An Analysis of U.S. Senate Elections*. Lanham, MD: Rowman & Littlefield.

Lau, Richard R. 1982. "Negativity in Person Perceptions." *Political Behavior* 4: 353-377.

Lau, Richard R. 1985. "Two Explanations for Negativity Effects in Political Behavior." *American Journal of Political Science* 29: 119-138.

Lau, Richard R. and David P. Redlawsk. 2001. "Advantages and Disadvantages of Cognitive Heuristics in Political Decision Making." *American Journal of Political Science* 45: 951-971.

Lau, Richard R. and Lee Sigleman. 2000. "Effectiveness of Negative Political Advertising." In James A. Thurber, Candice J. Nelson, and David A. Dulio, eds. *Crowded Airwaves: Campaign Advertising in Elections.* Washington, D.C.: Brookings Institution, 10-43.

Lau, Richard R. and David O. Sears, eds. 1986. *Political Cognition: The 19th Annual Carnegie Symposium on Cognition*. Hillsdale, N.J.: Lawrence Erlbaum.

Lau, Richard R., Lee Sigelman, and Ivy Brown Rovner. 2007. "The Effects of Negative Political Campaigns: A Meta-Analytic Reassessment." *The Journal of Politics* 69: 1176-1209.

Lazarsfeld, Paul F., Bernard Berelson, and Hazel Gaudet. 1944. *The People's Choice*. New York: Columbia University Press.

Leeper, Mark Stephen. 1991. "The Impact of Prejudice on Female Candidates: An Experimental Look at Voter Inference." *American Politics Quarterly* 19: 248-261.

Leibovich, Mark. 2008a. "Meanwhile, the Other No. 2 Keeps On Punching." *New York Times,* September 20, 2008.

Leibovich, Mark. 2008b. "Among Rock-Ribbed Fans of Palin, Dudes Rule." *The New York Times*, October 19.

Leibovich, Mark. 2012a. "On Stump in Ohio, Biden Attacks G.O.P. Rivals." *The New York Times*, March 16.

Leibovich, Mark. 2012b. "Obama Seizes Chance to Score as an Everyman." *The New York Times*, March 23.

Leibovich, Mark. 2012c. "For a Blunt Biden, an Uneasy Supporting Role." *The New York Times*, May 8.

Lewis-Beck, Michael S. 1989. *Economics and Elections*. Ann Arbor, MI: University of Michigan Press.

Lewis-Beck, Michael S. and Tom W. Rice. 1983. "Localism in Presidential Elections: The Home State Advantage." *American Journal of Political Science* 27: 548-556.

Liasson, Mara. 2008. "Effect of Vice Presidential Candidates Weighed." *National Public Radio*. September 12. Accessed February 7, 2012: http://www.npr.org/templates/story/story.php?storyId=94572481

Lida, Takeshi. 2005. "Does Negative Campaigning Reduce Uncertainty?" Paper Presented at the Annual Meeting of the Midwest Political Science Association.

Light, Paul C. 1984. *Vice-Presidential Power: Advice and Influence in the White House*. Baltimore, MD: Johns Hopkins University Press.

Lombard, Matthew, Jennifer Snyder-Duch, and Cheryl Campanella Bracken. 2002. "Content Analysis in Mass Communication: Assessment and Reporting of Intercoder Reliability." *Human Communication Research* 28: 587-604.

Lombard, Matthew, Jennifer Snyder-Duch, and Cheryl Campanella Bracken. 2010. "Practical Resources for Assessing and Reporting Intercoder Reliability in Content Analysis Research Projects." Accessed January 3, 2012: http://matthewlombard.com/reliability/

Lowery, Annie. 2012. "Conservative Elite in Capital Pay Heed to Ryan as a Thinker." *The New York Times*, August 18.

Malhortra, Neil and Jon A. Krosnick. 2007. "Retrospective and Prospective Performance Assessments During the 2004 Election Campaign: Tests of Mediation and News Media Priming." *Political Behavior* 29: 249-278.

Markus, Gregory B. 1982. "Political Attitudes During an Election Year: A Report on the 1980 NES Panel Study." *American Political Science Review* 76: 538-60.

Markus, Gregory B. 1988. "The Impact of Personal and National Economic Conditions on the Presidential Vote: A Pooled Cross-Sectional Analysis." *American Journal of Political Science* 32: 137-54.

Matland, Richard E. 1994. "Putting Scandinavian Equality to the Test: An Experimental Evaluation of Gender Stereotyping of Political Candidates in a Sample of Norwegian Voters." *British Journal of Political Science* 24: 273-292.

Matthews, Donald R. 1974. "Presidential Nominations: Process and Outcomes." In James D. Barber, ed. *Choosing the President*. Englewood Cliffs, N.J.: Prentice-Hall, 35-70.

Mayer, William G. 2000. "A Brief History of Vice Presidential Selection." In *In Pursuit of the White House 2000: How We Choose Our Presidential Nominees*. New York: Chatham House, 313-374.

McCarthy, Robert J. 2008. "Palin Unleashes Political Punches: In a Speech Full of Moxie, Veep Nominee Wallops Obama, Media, 'Elite.'" *Buffalo News*, September 4.

McCurley, Carl and Jeffrey J. Mondak. 1995. "Inspected by #1184063113: The Influence of Incumbents' Competence and Integrity in U.S. House Elections." *American Journal of Political Science* 39: 864-85.

McDermott, Monika L. 1997. "Voting Cues in Low-Information Elections: Candidate Gender as a Social Information Variable in Contemporary

United States Elections." *American Journal of Political Science* 41: 270-283.

McDermott, Monika L. 1998. "Race and Gender Cues in Low-Information Elections." *Political Research Quarterly* 51: 895- 918.

McDermott, Monika L. 2009. "Religious Stereotyping and Voter Support for Evangelical Candidates." *Political Research Quarterly* 62: 340-354.

McDonald, Jonathan Ladd and Gabriel S. Lentz. 2009. "Exploiting a Rare Shift to Document the Persuasive Power of the News Media." *American Journal of Political Science* 53: 394-410.

McGraw, Kathleen M. and Cristina Ling. 2003. "Media Priming of Presidential and Group Evaluations." *Political Communication* 20: 23-40.

McGraw, Kathleen M. 2003. "Political Impressions." In David O. Sears, Leonie Huddy, and Robert Jervis, eds. *Political Psychology*. Oxford: Oxford University Press, 394-432.

McGraw, Kathleen M. and Marco Steenbergen. 1997. "Pictures in the Head: Memory Representation of Political Candidates." In Milton Lodge and Kathleen M. McGraw, eds. *Political Judgment: Structure and Process*. Ann Arbor, MI: University of Michigan Press, 15-42.

McGuire, William J. 1968. "Personality and Susceptibility to Social Influence." In Edgar F. Borgatta and William W. Lambert, eds. *Handbook of Personality Theory and Research*. New York: Rand McNally, 1130-1187.

McGuire, William J. 1986. "The Myth of Massive Media Impact." In George Comstock, ed. *Public Communication and Behavior*. New York: Academic Press, 173-257.

Mendelsohn, M. 1996. "The Media and Interpersonal Communications: The Priming of Issues, Leaders, and Party Identification." *Journal of Politics* 58: 112-125.

Miller, Arthur H. and Warren E. Miller. 1976. "Ideology in the 1972 Election: Myth or Reality-A Rejoinder." *American Political Science Review* 70: 832-849.

Miller, Arthur H., Martin P. Wattenberg, and O. Malanchuk. 1986. "Schematic Assessments of Presidential Candidates." *American Political Science Review* 80: 521-540.

Miller, Joanne M. and Jon A. Krosnick. 2000. "News Media Impact on the Ingredients of Presidential Evaluations: Politically Knowledgeable Citizens are Guided by a Trusted Source." *American Journal of Political Science* 44: 295-309.

Miller, Warren E. and J. Merrill Shanks. 1982. "Policy Directions and Presidential Leadership: Alternative Interpretations of the 1980 Presidential Election." *British Journal of Political Science* 12: 299-356.

Miller, Warren E. and J. Merrill Shanks. 1996. *The New American Voter*. Cambridge, MA: Harvard University.

Mohr, Charles. 1984. "Nuclear First Use is Revived as Issue." *The New York Times,* September 9.

Mondak, Jeffrey J. 1995. "Competence, Integrity, and the Electoral Success of Congressional Incumbents." *Journal of Politics* 57: 1043-69.

Natoli, Marie D. 1985. American Prince, American Pauper: The Contemporary Vice Presidency in Perspective. Westport, CT: Greenwood Press.

Nelson, Michael. 1988. "Background Paper." In A Heartbeat Away: Report of the Twentieth Century Fund Task Force on the Vice Presidency. New York: Priority Press, 19-114.

Nelson, Michael. 1988. "Choosing the Vice President." *PS: Political Science and Politics* 21: 858-868.

Neuendorf, K. A. 2002. *The Content Analysis Guidebook.* Thousand Oaks, CA: Sage.

New York Times.com. 2009. "As Utility Player." *The New York Times Online,* March 29.

Newhagen, John E. and Byron Reeves. 1991. "Emotion and Memory Responses for Negative Political Advertising: A Study of Television Commercials Used in the 1988 Presidential Election." In Frank Biocca, ed. *Television and Political Advertising,* Vol. 1. Hillsdale, NJ: Lawrence Erlbaum, 197-220.

Nisbett, Richard E. and Lee Ross. 1980. *Human Inference: Strategies and Shortcomings of Social Judgment.* Englewood Cliffs, NJ: Prentice-Hall.

Niven, David. 2006. "A Field Experiment on the Effects of Negative Campaign Mail on Voter Turnout in a Municipal Election." *Political Research Quarterly* 59: 203-210.

Noelle-Neumann, Elisabeth. 1984. *The Spiral of Silence.* Chicago, IL: University of Chicago Press.

Noonan, Peggy. 2008. "Palin's Failin'." *Wall Street Journal,* October 17.

Nosek, Brian A., Frederick L. Smyth, Jeffrey J. Hansen, Thierry. Devos, Nicole M. Lindner, and Kate A. Ranganath. 2007. "Pervasiveness and Correlates of Implicit Attitudes and Stereotypes." *European Review of Social Psychology* 18: 36–88.

Olson, Michael A. and Russell H. Fazio. 2003. "Relations between Implicit Measures of Prejudice: What are we Measuring?" *Psychological Science* 14: 636-639.

Oreskes, Michael. 1984. "Meeting of Three Candidates and O'Connot Stirs a Debate." *The New York Times,* November 3.

Ottati, Victor C. and Robert S. Wyer Jr. 1990. "The Cognitive Mediators of Political Choice: Toward a Comprehensive Model of Political Information Processing." In John A. Ferejohn and James H. Kuklinski, eds. *Information and Democratic Processes.* Chicago, IL: University of Illinois Press, 186-216.

Page, Benjamin I. 1978. Choices and Echoes in Presidential Elections: Rational Man and Electoral Democracy. Chicago, IL: University of Chicago Press.

Pantoja, Adrian D. and Gary M. Segura. 2003. "Does Ethnicity Matter? Descriptive Representation in Legislatures and Political Alienation Among Latinos." *Social Science Quarterly* 84: 441-460.

Paolino, Phillip. 1995. "Group-Salient Issues and Group Representation: Support for Women Candidates in the 1992 Senate Elections." *American Journal of Political Science* 39: 294- 313.

Parker, Kathleen. 2012. "Marco Rubio has What Mitt Romney Needs in a Vice President." *Washington Post,* January 3.

Patterson, Thomas C. 1980. *The Mass Media Election.* New York: Praeger.

Paul, David and Jessi L. Smith. 2008. "Subtle Sexism? Examining Vote Preferences When Women Run Against Men for the Presidency." *Journal of Women, Politics, and Policy* 29: 451-476.

Payne, B. Keith, Jon A. Krosnick, Josh Pasek, Yphtach Lelkes, Omair Akhtar, and Trevor Tompson. 2010. "Implicit and Explicit Prejudice in the 2008 American Presidential Election." *Journal of Experimental Social Psychology* 46: 367-374.

Perlez, Jane. 1984a. "Ferraro Wraps it Up at Marymount." *New York Times*, November 6.

Perlez, Jane. 1984b. "Ferraro Says Religion Won't Influence Policy." *The New York Times,* September 13.

Perlez, Jane. 1984c. "Ferraro Dogged by Queries on Family." *The New York Times,* October 27.

Perlez, Jane. 1984d. "Ferraro Returns to City and Hometown Cheers." *The New York Times,* October 23.

Perlez, Jane. 1984e. "'Certain Things, Phil, Are Personal,' Ferraro Says." *The New York Times,* October 31.

Perez-Pena, Richard. 2000. "The 2000 Campaign: Lieberman Revisits Faith's Role in U.S." *The New York Times*, October 25.

Perreault, William D. and Laurence E. Leigh. 1989. "Reliability of Nominal Data Based on Qualitative Judgments." *Journal of Marketing Research* 26: 135-148.

Peters, Jeremy W. 2012. "Limited Convention Broadcasts Shut Out Ann Romney." *The New York Times*, August 23.

Peterson, David A.M. 2009. "Campaign Learning and Vote Determinants." *American Journal of Political Science* 53: 445-460.

Philips, Kate. 2008. "In One Country, Gusts of Change." *The New York Times,* November 2.

Pierce, Patrick A. 1993. "Political Sophistication and the Use of Candidate Traits in Candidate Evaluation." *Political Psychology* 14: 21-35.

Polsby, Nelson W. and Aaron Wildavsky. 2012. *Presidential Elections: Strategies and Structures of American Politics,* 12th ed. Lanham, MD. Rowman & Littlefield Publishers, Inc.

Pomper, George. 1966. "The Nomination of Hubert Humphrey for Vice-President." *Journal of Politics* 28: 639-659.

Pomper, Gerald. 1963. *Nominating the President.* Evanston, IL: Northwestern University Press.

Popkin, Samuel L. 1991. The Reasoning Voter: Communication and Persuasion in Presidential Campaigns. Chicago, IL: University of Chicago Press.

Popping, Roel. 1988. "On Agreement for Nominal Data." In Willem E. Saris and Irmtraud N. Gallhofer, eds. *Sociometric Research: Volume 1, Data Collection and Scaling.* New York: St. Martin's Press, pp. 90-105.

Potter, W. James and Deborah Levine-Donnerstein. 1999. "Rethinking Validity and Reliability in Content Analysis." *Journal of Applied Communication Research* 27: 258-284.

Powell, Michael. 2008. "Democrats in Steel Country See Skin Color, and Beyond It." *New York Times*, October 27.

PR Newswire. 2008. "Sarah Palin Generates More Search Interest than Hurricane Gustav and the DNC Combined, Seeing Biggest Bump in Search Activity on Lycos." September 4.

Pratto, Felicia and Oliver P. John. 1991. "Automatic Vigilance: The Attention-Grabbing Power of Negative Social Information." *Journal of Personality and Social Psychology* 61: 380-391.

Prior, Markus. 2009a. "Improving Media Effects Research through Better Measurement of News Exposure." *The Journal of Politics* 71: 893-908.

Prior, Markus. 2009b. "The Immensely Inflated News Audience: Assessing Bias in Self-Reported News Exposure." *Public Opinion Quarterly* 73: 130-143.

Ragsdale, Lyn. 1997. "Disconnected Politics: Public Opinion and Presidents." In Barbara Norrander and Clyde Wilcox, eds. *Understanding Public Opinion*. Washington, DC: CQ Press, 229-251.

Rahn, Wendy M. 1993. "The Role of Partisan Stereotypes in Information Processing about Political Candidates." *American Journal of Political Science* 37: 472-96.

Rahn, Wendy M., John H. Aldrich, Eugene Borgida, and John L. Sullivan. 1990. "A Social-Cognitive Model of Candidate Appraisal." In John A. Ferejohn and James H. Kuklinski, eds. *Information and Democratic Processes*. Urbana, IL: University of Illinois Press, 136-159.

Raines, Howell. 1984. "Bush and Ferraro Debate; Disagree about Leadership, Foreign Policy, and Religion." *The New York Times,* October 12.

Raines, Howell. 2000. "Editorial Observer; When Devotion Counts More than Doctrine." *The New York Times,* September 17.

Richey, Marjorie H., Frank S. Bono, Helen V. Lewis, and Harold W. Richey. 1982. "Selectivity of Negativity Bias in Impression Formation." *Journal of Social Psychology* 116: 107-118.

Richmond, Rose. 2008. "Why John McCain and Sarah Palin Lost this Election." *Yahoo! Voices.* November 6. Accessed February 7, 2012: http://voices.yahoo.com/why-john-mccain-sarah-palin-lost-election-2150306.html

Riggle, Ellen D., Victor Ottati, Robert S. Wyer, James Kuklinski, and Norbert Schwartz. 1992. "Bases of Political Judgments: The Role of Stereotypic and Nonstereotypic Information." *Political Behavior* 14: 67-87.

Roberts, Marilyn S. 1995. "Political Advertising: Strategies for Influence." In Kathleen E. Kendall, ed. *Presidential Campaign Discourse: Strategic Communication Problems*. Albany, NY: SUNY Press, 179-99.

Roberts, Sam. 1984. "Judge Approves Set of Guidelines on Conservators." *The New York Times,* November 6.

Robinson, John. 1974. "Perceived Media Bias and the 1968 Vote." *Journalism Quarterly* 49: 239-246.

Rohde, David W. 1991. *Parties and Leaders in the Postreform House*. Chicago, IL: University of Chicago Press.

Rohter, Larry. 1992. "The 1992 Campaign: Candidate's Wife; Unrepentant, Marilyn Quayle Fights for Family and Values." *The New York Times,* October 28.

Romero, David W. 2004. "Requiem for a Lightweight: Vice Presidential Candidate Evaluations and the Presidential Vote." *Presidential Studies Quarterly* 31: 454-463.

Rosenstone, Steven J. 1983. *Forecasting Presidential Elections*. New Haven, CT: Yale University Press.

Rosenthal, Andrew. 1991. "On My Mind; A Change for Quayle." *The New York Times,* May 7.

Rosenthal, Andrew. 1992. "The 1992 Campaign: Issues – 'Family Values'; Bush Tries to Recoup from Harsh Tone on 'Values.'" *The New York Times,* September 21.

Rosenwasser, Shirley M. and Jana Seale. 1988. "Attitudes Toward a Hypothetical Male or Female Presidential Candidate: A Research Note." *Political Psychology* 9: 591-598.

Rosenwasser, Shirley M. and Norma G. Dean. 1989. "Gender Role and Political Office." *Psychology of Women Quarterly* 13: 77-85.

Rossiter, Clinton L. 1948. "The Reform of the Vice Presidency." *Political Studies Quarterly* 63: 383-403.

Sack, Kevin. 1992. "The 1992 Campaign: The Vice President; Quayle Tries to Separate Family Values and 'Murphy Brown.'" *The New York Times,* September 3.

Safire, William. 1992. "On Language: Family Values." *The New York Times,* September 6.

Sanbonmatsu, Kira. 2002: "Gender Stereotypes and Vote Choice." *American Journal of Political Science* 46: 20-34.

Sanger, David E. 2009. "Pakistan an Early Test of Obama's Approach." *The New York Times*, January 27.

Sapiro, Virginia. 1981-1982. "If U.S. Senator Baker Were a Woman: An Experimental Study of Candidate Images." *Political Psychology* 2: 61-83.

Schuman, Howard, Charlotte Steeh, Lawrence Bobo, and Maria Krysan. 1997. *Racial Attitudes in America: Trends and Interpretations.* Cambridge, MA: Harvard University Press.

Seelye, Katharine Q. 2008. "Though an Experienced Debater, Biden Often Tripped up by Sponteneity." *New York Times*, October 1.

Seun, Hoi K. and Patrick S.C. Lee. 1985. "Effects of the Use of Percentage Agreement on Behavior Observation Reliabilities: A Reassessment." *Journal of Psychopathy and Behavioral Assessment* 7: 21-234.

Shanks, J. Merrill, and Warren E. Miller. 1990. "Policy Direction and Performance Evaluation: Complementary Explanations of the Reagan Elections." *British Journal of Political Science* 20: 143-235.

Shanks, J. Merrill, and Warren E. Miller. 1991. "Partisanship, Policy, and Performance: The Reagan Legacy in the 1988 Election." *British Journal of Political Science* 21: 129-97.

Shaw, Daron R. 1999. "The Effect of TV Ads and Candidate Appearances on Statewide Presidential Votes, 1988-1996." *American Political Science Review* 93: 345-61.

Shaw, Daron R. and James G.Gimpel. 2012. "What if We Randomize the Governor's Schedule? Evidence on Campaign Appearance Effects From a Texas Field Experiment." *Political Communication* 29: 137-159.

Sigelman, Lee and Paul J. Wahlbeck. 1997. "The 'Veepstakes': Strategic Choice in Presidential Running Mate Selection." *American Political Science Review* 91: 855-864.

Sigelman, Carol K., Lee Sigelman, Barbara J. Walkosz, and Michael Nitz. 1995. "Black Candidates, White Voters: Understanding Racial Bias in Political Perceptions." *American Journal of Political Science* 39: 243-65

Silverman, Fran. 2008. "Economy Voters' Top Worry, But Agreement Stops There." *The New York Times,* October 26.

Simon, Adam F. 2002. The Winning Message: Candidate Behavior, Campaign Discourse, and Democracy. New York: Cambridge University Press.

Simon, Herbert A. 1957. *Models of Man: Social and Rational.* New York: Wiley.

Simon, Herbert A. 1985. "Human Nature in Politics: The Dialogue of Psychology with Political Science." *American Political Science Review* 79: 293-304.

Singletary, Michael W. 1993. Mass Communication Research: Contemporary Methods and Applications. Boston, MA: Addison-Wesley.

Smith, Jessi L., David Paul, and Rachel Paul. 2007. "No Place for a Woman: Evidence for Gender Bias in Evaluations of Presidential Candidates." *Basic and Applied Social Psychology* 29: 225-33.

Stanley, Alessandra. 2009. "The Vanishing Sidekick." *The New York Times,* March 8.

Stempel, Guido H. 1952. "Sample Size for Classifying Subject Matter in Dailies." *Journalism Quarterly* 29: 333-334.

Stevens, Daniel. 2005. "The Two Routes for Effects of Negative Advertising." Paper Presented at the Annual Meeting of the Midwest Political Science Association.

Stevens, Daniel. 2009. "Elements of Negativity: Volume and Proportion in Exposure to Negative Advertising." *Political Behavior* 31: 429-445.

Stimson, James A. 2004. *Tides of Consent*. New York: Cambridge University Press.

Stoker, Laura. 1993. "Judging Presidential Character: The Demise of Gary Hart." *Political Behavior* 15: 193-223.

Stokes, Donald E. 1966. "Some Dynamic Elements of Contests for the Presidency." *The American Political Science Review* 60: 19–28.

Stolberg, Sheryl Gay. 2010. "A Latter-Day Happy Warrior Tries to Energize Democrats." *The New York Times*, October 13.

Strauss, Daniel. 2012. "Ryan: I've got more experience on foreign policy than '08 Obama." *The Hill,* August 21. Accessed September 17, 2012: http://64.147.104.30/blogs/blog-briefing-room/news/244613-paul-ryan-i-have-a-lot-more-foreign-policy-experience-than-obama-when-he-became-president

Sulfaro, Valerie A. 1998. "Political Sophistication and the Presidential Campaign: Citizen Reactions to Campaign Advertisements." *Paper Presented at the Annual Meeting of the Midwest Political Science Association.*

Taber, Charles S. and Milton Lodge. 2006. "Motivated Skepticism in the Evaluation of Political Beliefs." *American Journal of Political Science* 50: 755-769.

Tate, Katherine. 1993. *From Protest to Politics*. Cambridge, MA: Harvard University Press and the Russell Sage Foundation.

Tate, Katherine. 2001. "The Political Representation of Blacks in Congress: Does Race Matter?" *Legislative Studies Quarterly* 26: 623-38.

The Richmonder. 2008. "Will Sarah Palin Destroy the Republican Party?" November 6.

Thurber, James A., Candice J. Nelson, and David A. Dulio, eds. 2000. *Crowded Airwaves: Campaign Advertising in Elections*. Washington, D.C.: Brookings Institution.

Tinsley, Howard E. A. and David J. Weiss. 2000. "Interrater Reliability and Agreement." In Howard E.A. Tinsley and Stephen D. Brown, eds. *Handbook of Applied Multivariate Statistics and Mathematical Modeling*. San Diego, CA: Academic Press, 95-124.

Turque, Bill, Michael Isikoff, Mark Hosenball, Matt Bai, and John Barry. 2000. "The Soul and the Steel." *Newsweek*, August 21.

Wang, Xiaopeng and Daniel Riffe. 2010. "An Exploration of Sample Sizes for Content Analysis of the New York Times Web Site." *The Web Journal of Mass Communication Research,* Vol. 20. Accessed January 3, 2012: http://www.scripps.ohiou.edu/wjmcr/vol20/

Watson, Robert P. and Richard M. Yon. 2006. "Vice Presidential Selection in the Modern Era." *White House Studies* 6: 163–78.

Wattenberg, Martin 1995. "The Role of Vice-Presidential Candidate Ratings in Presidential Voting Behavior." *American Politics Quarterly* 23: 504-14.

Wattenberg, Martin. 1984. "And Tyler, Too." *Public Opinion* 7: 52-54.

West, Darrell M. 1991. "Television and Presidential Popularity in America." *British Journal of Political Science* 21: 199-214.

Williams, Irving G. 1956. *The Rise of the Vice-Presidency* Washington: Public Affairs Press.

Williams, Linda E. 1990. "White/Black Perceptions of the Electability of Black Political Candidates." In Lucius J. Barker, ed. *Black Electoral Politics*. New Brunswick, NJ: Transaction, 45-64.

Wimmer, Roger D. and Joseph R. Dominick. 1991. *Mass Media Research: An Introduction,* 3d ed. Belmont, CA: Wadsworth.

Wines, Michael. 1992. "Views on Single Motherhood are Multiple at White House." *The New York Times,* May 21.

Witcover, Jules. 1977. Marathon: The Pursuit of the Presidency, 1972-1976. New York: Viking Press.

Wlezien, Christopher and Robert S. Erikson. 2001. "Campaign Effects in Theory and Practice." *American Politics Research* 29: 419-36.

Wlezien, Christopher and Robert S. Erikson. 2002. "The Time Line of Presidential Election Campaigns." *Journal of Politics* 64: 969-93.

Yardley, William. 2008. "Husband of Alaska Governor Refuses to Testify in Legislature's Trooper Inquiry." *The New York Times,* September 19.

Zaller, John. 1987. "Diffusion of Political Attitudes." *Journal of Personality and Social Psychology* 53: 821-833.

Zaller, John. 1989. "Bringing Converse Back: Modeling Information Flow in Political Campaigns." *Political Analysis* 1: 181-234.

Zaller, John R. 1992. *The Nature and Origins of Mass Opinion.* New York: Cambridge University Press.

Zaller, John. 1996. "The Myth of Massive Media Impact Revived: New Support for a Discredited Idea." In Diane Mutz, Paul Sniderman, and Richard Brody, eds. *Political Persuasion and Attitude Change.* Ann Arbor, MI: University of Michigan Press, 17-78.

Zernike, Kate and Kim Severson. 2008. "A Low-Key Outdoorsman and Family Man Now Faces a National Role." *The New York Times,* September 3.

Index

About the Book

Do vice presidential candidates play any significant role in presidential elections? Challenging the conventional wisdom, Stacy Ulbig shows the important ways in which they do in fact affect election outcomes. She also assesses the impact of a range of vice presidential candidates and considers how the news media fits in the equation. Analyzing data from 1972 through 2008, Ulbig shows clearly how and why vice presidents matter in presidential campaigns.

Stacy G. Ulbig is associate professor of political science at Sam Houston State University.